Andrew,
Thanks for being
good to Livy man,
This book will get
you anything in life

Brett D.

Behavioral Karma™

The 5 SCIENTIFIC Laws Of Life
& Leadership

Brett DiNovi and Paul Gavoni

Brett DiNovi & Associates

BEHAVIORAL KARMA™

Copyright ©2020 Brett DiNovi International

Disclaimers:
The publisher and the author make no guarantees concerning the level of success you may experience by following the advice and strategies contained in this book, and you accept the risk that results will differ for each individual. The testimonials and examples provided in this book show exceptional results, which may not apply to the average reader, and are not intended to represent or guarantee that you will achieve the same or similar results. If expert assistance or counseling is needed, the services of a competent professional should be sought. Neither the publisher nor authors shall be liable for any personal loss or commercial damages, including, but not limited to special, incidental, consequential, or other damages.

ISBN: 978-1-7352557-0-5

DEDICATION

This book is dedicated to those
who wish to make a positive difference in their life
and the lives of others

Table of Contents

Acknowledgments

Brett

First and foremost, I would like to thank Marlene Selfridge, the love of my life, who is the reason I was inspired to come out of the dark place I was in back in 2011. Marlene's unconditional love brought my passion out enabling me to use these 5 laws of life and leadership to climb back from bankruptcy, insurmountable IRS debt, and divorce. I was also equally inspired by my daughter, Olivia Paige DiNovi, to make this uphill journey and rebuild my relationship with her after years I felt a lack of purpose. My two stepsons Justin Selfridge and Benjamin Selfridge also made it all worth it to rebuild a new family unit.

I would also like to thank my good friend and colleague Paulie Gavoni for the patience he demonstrated with my procrastination while writing this book. Paulie used behavioral science to push me through my writer's block by breaking it down into small segments and positively reinforcing my work with his highly desirable social attention. I'm thankful for my mother Brunhild Seeger DiNovi who always had faith in me during the most difficult periods of my life and my late father Jack DiNovi who instilled discipline and focus in me in my earlier years wrestling.

I must also thank my good friend and accountant Salvatore Giampapa for guiding me with business advice during those difficult times when most other professionals had given up on me. Lastly, I'm thankful for Jason Golowski, our Chief Strategy Officer, that implemented these 5 laws of life and leadership numerous times and adapted them for a drastically different culture up in the state of Maine.

Paulie

I would like to thank my parents, John and Susan Parry, and Paul Gavoni, for providing their continued unconditional love and support while teaching me to value being kind, compassionate and helpful to people regardless of race, religion, gender, etc. You have been amazing role models for me. I would also like to thank my beautiful wife, Nikki Gavoni, and my brilliant and wonderful son, Niko Gavoni, for their unyielding support and many sacrifices that have allowed me to focus a considerable portion of my time and energy to this manuscript. I love you all very, *very* much.

We would also like to thank our work family, who directly contributed to this book. These amazing behavioral ambassadors include Bernie Baugh, Erin Bertoli, Billy Brown, Anika Costa, Jason Golowski, Kate Harrison, Joe Kendorski, Jess Kreppel, Matt Linder, Stefanie Perrin, Manny Rodriguez, and Amanda Wolf. In addition to these good folks, there are many people who have directly or indirectly had a positive impact on us. Unfortunately, we'd have to write an entirely separate book just to recognize everybody who invested in us. But we want you all to know we love and are thankful for you. This is your book as much as it is ours!

SECTION I

The Science of Helping

CHAPTER 1

Introduction

L ife has provided us with many challenges. Victims of bullying as children, we both struggled with our own sense of self. Fortunately, we each found combat sports and used them as a springboard to develop confidence or grit that would see us through a number of dark times, including depression, anxiety, death, and bankruptcy. As former combat athletes and coaches, we will use some combat sports analogies throughout this book, as we see many aspects of life and leadership as a struggle. A fight. And like the famous fictional character, Rocky Balboa said, "You, me, or nobody is gonna hit as hard as life. But it ain't about how hard you hit. It's about how hard you can get hit and keep moving forward; how much you can take and keep moving forward." Life is not a fight in the literal sense, of course, but in the sense that we must each learn to navigate obstacles and overcome adversity if we are going to move toward who and what we value. There is a science for navigating these obstacles that will allow you to improve behavior, performance, and achieve desired outcomes. This science, the science of human behavior, is frequently misunderstood or misrepresented. But it is real and it is highly effective, and the practical application of the technologies can make an immediate and lasting difference in your life and the lives of others.

Our first exposure to the science of human behavior was what leading researcher and professor of psychology Dr. Richard Foxx (1996) called the *"Aha!" experience,* as we quickly realized we now had a conceptual framework that explained how we had been approaching things our whole lives. We found that the strategies, methods, and procedures we gravitated toward had names and a scientific basis. The basic principles just made sense to us, and we know there are those of you out there like us who will feel the same. In the 1996 article titled, "Translating the Covenant: The Behavior Analyst as Ambassador and Translator," Dr. Foxx called people like us "natural behavior analysts," as our approach feels almost instinctual or intuitive when solving problems and decision making.

Since that time, we have been fortunate enough to use science to help thousands of children with disabilities, parents, students, teachers, principals, and organizational managers and leaders achieve various valued outcomes. From turning around failing schools and developing champion athletes to building and leading an organization from zero to eight figures, we have always been passionate about helping people achieve valued outcomes. Given that we are armed with what we believe to be the most powerful toolbox in the world for improving performance and helping people reach desired outcomes, we feel we cannot go wrong in sharing the five powerful laws and supportive behavior hacks outlined in this book for improving life and leadership. Incidentally, a *hack*, for those of you don't know, can be characterized as "an appropriate application of ingenuity." Perhaps one might even consider a *behavior hack* "a clever approach." *A behavior hack,* therefore, might be considered "a clever approach to applying scientific and lawful principles of behavior to achieving positive outcomes." And our book is chock full of the practical application of behavior science for making a positive difference in your life and the lives of others.

Behavioral Karma and the 5 Scientific Laws

Karma, an ancient term thrown around for thousands of years, has become kind of a buzzword in our current culture often reflected in idioms like, "You reap what you sow," or, "What goes around comes around." The *Spiritual Encyclopedia* (n.d.) has this to say about karma:

> It's a Sanskrit word meaning 'act,' 'action,' or 'word.' The law of karma teaches us that all of our thoughts, words and actions begin a chain of cause and effect and that we will personally experience the effects of everything we cause. We may not experience the effect (the returning karma) right away, and it may not even be in this lifetime, but you can count on it just the same. It is a cosmic law, which means that it applies to everyone, everywhere, all the time. This law exists entirely for our own good. It allows us to make progress in our soul's evolution. As you know, the things we think, say and do can be positive or negative. In the same way, karma can be positive or negative.

Moreover, Open College UK Website (n.d.) states, "All human thoughts which lead to words and expressions or output and consequently behavior onto others create a ripple or a wave, and this can be called *energy* whether you believe it or not."

Now, to our knowledge, there is no scientific evidence that supports the existence of a "cosmic law" or a "soul's evolution" that produces energy. But there are the laws of human behavior and a science that supports that thoughts, words, and actions do have a cause and effect. That is, your behavior and the behavior of others produce consequences that directly impact the likelihood that you or others will engage in that behavior again. And since most of us behave around others, our behavior is often impacting them, and their behavior is often impacting us. For the purpose of this book, these numerous interlocking behaviors form a *metacontigency* (Glenn, 1988) or a series of "if-thens" that result in almost a ripple effect between and across people through time and space, what we call *behavioral karma*. Now, through a scientific perspective, this phenomenon can be explained succinctly through good behavior analysis. But we are guessing that you didn't pick up this book to be inundated with scientific terminology, some of which we even struggle with! You are likely reading it because you'd like to learn some simple, evidence-based approaches for making a positive difference in your life and the lives of those around you. As such, we do our best to pair scientific language and principles with everyday language so that the concepts make sense. For example, while the term *karma* is clearly not scientific, we are pairing it with behavior and its impact between and across persons, as most people have the general understanding that karma is associated with reciprocation and a ripple effect.

In this book you will find that most behavior is functional or serves a purpose, and in a sense, has karma since something occurs as a result of it. When a person or people behave differently in response to your behavior and this results in meaningful outcomes for them and those around them (this includes you), we call that *positive behavioral karma*. If this consequence is not valued or even aversive, your behavior and the behavior of others will occur just long enough to avoid something unpleasant and likely stop once that unpleasant thing is avoided or removed. This type of consequence might be thought of as *negative behavioral karma*. Though positive and negative have different meanings in the science, as we discussed above, for the purpose of this book, it's easiest just to think about positive and negative as most people already do. That is, positive (good) outcomes occur as a result of behavior, or negative (bad) outcomes occur as a result. And because the behavior of people is often interlocking, you and others might experience *instant behavioral karma* (e.g., you smile at somebody, they smile back; you yell at somebody, they yell back) or *delayed behavioral karma* (e.g., you help somebody now, they help you later; a manager talks down to an employee, they produce less and eventually quit). We'll further unpack the concept of behavioral karma in chapter 2. What's important to understand is that there can be a ripple effect of behavior change that occurs as a result of the consequences produced by your behavior, and the behavior of others. This ripple effect produced by your behavior, or behavioral karma, can occur across individuals, groups, and organizations and can be succinctly explained and reproduced through a simple understanding of the scientific principles of human behavior.

Across each chapter, we have captured the essence of *behavioral karma* and the underlying behavioral science for achieving success in life and leadership through what we call *the 5 scientific laws*. The Merriam-Webster (n.d.) Dictionary defines a *law* as "a statement of an order or relation of phenomena that so far as is known is invariable under the given conditions." There is no doubt that what we present in this book is "invariable under the given conditions," as the laws presented are based on behavioral science. We have found that these 5 laws have allowed us to build successful performance across organizations and produce positive outcomes in every facet of our personal and professional lives. Sometimes, when we or others fail to reach success, people tend to blame. It's easy to blame others.

If that's all it took to be successful, many people would be extremely prosperous. Instead of blaming, we regularly use the laws to more accurately assess and then precisely isolate problems that prevent us or others from being successful. And then we relentlessly use the 5 laws to help produce positive and meaningful outcomes. While we will unpack each of the scientific laws and provide concrete examples through a variety of behavior hacks, we want to foreshadow things to come with a brief description of them.

Pinpointing

The first law is *pinpointing*. When we say pinpointing, we mean (a) *pinpointing* the problem, (b) pinpointing the result or outcome, and (c) pinpointing the actions that resolve the problem and achieve the desired outcome, what result you want to achieve, and precisely what actions must be taken to achieve it. Knowing exactly what needs to be done allows you to pinpoint problems when results are not achieved. Then, pinpointing just one or two actions can result in the biggest impact related to the problem. This can be the one or two things you can do or the one or two things that can be done at scale.

Goal Setting

The next law is *goal setting*. Most of us understand it can be difficult to mobilize people and do anything without a clear goal. But a powerful behavior hack is to develop goals and then shift them to accomplishments as leading indicators of progress toward the goal. You will learn more about the power of accomplishments for achieving goals. But for now, please know that this simple shift can have a huge influence on performance and goal attainment.

Self-Monitoring and Report Out

Then there is *the law of self-monitoring and report out*. Once you've pinpointed actions and established goals, self-monitoring and report out becomes a powerful source of data, motivation, and saliency of progress toward goals. It allows for you, or others, to start removing excuses by isolating and assessing behavior and results. One of the key points to self-monitoring is reporting out the data to somebody else. When you or the folks in your circle or organization know that progress must be reported to someone else, it can have a profound effect on both motivation and the development and refinement of critical habits. It also embeds accountability.

Reciprocal Feedback

The fourth law is related to feedback. Specifically, *reciprocal feedback*. "You good?" "Ya, I'm good ... how about you?" While it may not seem like rocket science, it is behavioral science. All learning requires feedback. We all need it, regardless of our position on an organizational chart, within a team, or perhaps within your own household. But often we fail to obtain feedback on our performance. How often has a parent said to their child, "Hey, how is my parenting?" or perhaps a leader asked their employees, "How do you feel about my leadership?" By giving and recruiting feedback from others, a loop can be created that has a powerful effect on our behavior and the behavior of others. Hence the need for reciprocal feedback.

Pay for Performance

The final law is to *pay for performance*. Pay for performance in an organization might seem obvious. Now, in life, pay for performance is different. For example, you know you don't earn cash for being nice to your spouse. But being "paid" depends on how you look at it. Is your spouse happier as a result? Are you happier? Does it increase the quality of life for you and your family? If it does, this might be considered positive behavioral karma. So it really depends on how you look at it. The bottom line is this: There must be "skin in the game" if you or anybody else are to engage in the day-to-day behavior that will achieve desired outcomes. When there is no value, there is typically no behavior. When there is little value, there is typically little behavior. And when there is great value, there is typically a lot of behavior. In the science, we call this phenomenon the "matching law," as people will behave proportionately to the amount of reinforcement (more on this later) the behavior produces.

Whenever we have a performance-based issue, we just keep looking at the problem, the environment, and detaching the person from it. We avoid blaming. Instead, we approach the problem through the lens of the 5 laws. And when planning any projects, whether they be personal or professional, we use the 5 laws to increase the likelihood of success for ourselves and those around us. Throughout most of the book, we use our collective voice to share knowledge and mutual experiences. However, at times you will note we break off into a personal story and switch from the we voice to an I voice. We believe this will help our book remain as authentic as possible through our very personal experiences; moreover, we believe it pumps life into critical concepts through various events we deem impactful and meaningful to the book. Finally, we believe people tend to learn best from multiple exemplars.

The Science of Helping

We very much value helping people, helping people help themselves, and helping people help others. And we believe the science of human behavior is the greatest tool for making this happen. We don't believe out of blind faith as a disciple might, but rather as a result of the consistent application and achievement of outcomes using the laws outlined in this book. We strongly believe the concepts and behavior hacks shared in our book can improve leadership and the lives of anybody, anywhere, to achieve desired outcomes across settings and conditions. The science of human behavior is the greatest science in the world. As behavior analysts, we are clearly biased. But case in point: What other science has the ability to improve other sciences by accelerating the performance of the scientists in their respective fields? Even scientists from other fields are beginning to recognize behavioral science as a solution to global problems and that it is directly linked to changes in human behavior (Ledoux, 2014). There are even calls for the replacement of chief executive officers with chief behavior officers, as the success of any organization is dependent on behavior—the behavior of leaders, the behavior of employees and the behavior of consumers.

So what does this mean for you? In short, opportunity. That is, an opportunity for you to behave in ways that make a positive difference in your life and the lives of others. If you are interested in improving performance, achieving goals, and helping yourself and others move toward the people and things valued, read on!

KEY TAKEAWAYS:

- » Behavioral karma is simply the impact of behavior between and across people.
- » There are principles rooted in the science of human behavior that explain what you do, and what others do.
- » There are principles rooted in the science of human behavior that explain this impact.
- » A behavior hack is a clever approach to applying the lawful principles of behavior to achieve meaningful outcomes.
- » It's not about blame, it's about behavior.
- » Anybody can leverage the principles of human behavior to make a positive and lasting difference in their life and the lives of others.

ASK YOURSELF:

- » What goals have you established that you've failed to achieve?
- » Are you aware of the root causes of issues you may be struggling with?
- » Are you aware of the impact of your behavior on yourself? How do you know?

CHAPTER 2

From the Bottom to the Top

Before we dig deeper into the 5 laws, we want to further set the stage by providing you a better understanding of what behavioral karma and the 5 laws actually look like in life and leadership. And while we will use a personal story of failure and success, try not to get caught up in the context. The principles of human behavior, as captured in the 5 laws, are applicable everywhere there are people. From your home to your work, to every state, country, continent, and culture, the same exact behavioral principles are at work. Like gravity, they are everywhere. Okay, let's cue the Hollywood special effects as we travel back in time.

Failure to Fortune—Brett's Story

> As I woke up in the bus station in Atlantic City, New Jersey, and noticed my pockets were empty (they weren't when I fell asleep!), I was happy to see my laptop computer and phone were still there, although the $20 I had left in my pocket definitely had been stolen. I was in New Jersey, don't forget. I looked at the screen saver on my phone, where I saw a picture of my daughter and my angel Marlene, who I hoped would one day allow me back into her home. While they both were the ladies of my life, I had not seen them in quite some time. The fault was mine. The reason—my behavior.

Now, you might be thinking, how in the hell did you get there in the first place? I've asked myself that very same question. The first thing that comes to mind here is that my wrestling career in 1988 had me at the world-class Olympic level; however, being plagued with injuries after getting a full ride and only being able to complete four out of five years in Division 1 college at West Virginia University (WVU) was one of the hardest things I'd ever faced. What I took out of this was that a bad situation can help you refocus your energy to succeed in other areas. So when I realized I could never recapture the world-class success near the end of my undergraduate work, I went all in studying behavior analysis to try to be the best at one thing. I hunted down Drs. Julie and Ernest Vargas [daughter and son-in-law of Dr. B. F. Skinner] with the tenacity to learn as much as I could while still on a full ride at WVU. If I didn't have a full ride, I would never have been able to afford to go to WVU. I suspect it was the harnessing of the tenacity and desire to achieve the world-class success that made me fortunate enough for both Julie and Ernie to take me under their wings and allow me to teach the Intro to Behaviorology course, a rare opportunity for a first-year grad student. This paid for my graduate school all three years.

Unfortunately, as the result of my continued pursuit of world-class success in wrestling, I had injured my shoulder again, and again, and again. It wasn't long before I noticed my father's time, attention, and visits to WVU to see me begin to wane, and then suddenly stop when I was unable to compete in wrestling. To cope with the pain and disappointment, I ended up drinking and partying while injured. Mind you, this was for 80 percent of my undergraduate years! When I entered graduate school, I was so excited to share with my father what I was accomplishing by teaching an applied behavior analysis class and studying under B. F. Skinner's daughter. I had hoped he'd be excited as well, and it would rekindle our relationship. Sadly, that didn't seem to interest my father as much as wrestling. In my father's defense, he was going through a lot and was just ending his career and beginning his retirement, which can be a tough phase in somebody's life. I presume that my father never refocused his energy toward a hobby or interest after his retirement because, within one week of retirement, his health deteriorated. In fact, right after retirement, he had a brain aneurysm that left him unable to speak, walk or use the bathroom. He was essentially in a coma for a week. I deserted pursuing my doctorate at WVU and rushed back to New Jersey to help my father recover. I was grateful that what I learned in graduate school from Julie about fluency and precision teaching was directly applicable to my father's rehabilitation. The part of my father's brain that was damaged did not allow him to recall anything from his short-term memory. But after rigorous, repeated precision teaching and fluency drills with flashcards, my father gradually regained important facts that kept him safe. This included things like his phone number, what to tell a security guard if he was lost by reciting his home address, and many other details that he could never have retrieved without this powerful teaching technology of applied behavior analysis.

But while I regularly applied the science to help others in personal and professional life as a behavior analyst, I failed to live and breathe the principles in my daily living. Eventually, the drinking and partying that I began engaging in as band-aid in college, caught up to me. Where it began as my crutch, my best friend, it ended up being my ultimate downfall. My frustrations, fueled by addictions, resulted in the use of my wrestling skills in the worst ways possible. Despite my problems, I always felt the need to stick up for victims of bullying. Many situations occurred where my judgment was clouded. For example, one night, I was playing pool in a tavern, and my friend and I were being verbally bullied by a large man who ended up taking a swing at me over a simple pool game. This 250-pound man would have buried me if he landed this punch, so I resorted to my wrestling skills and took the man down with a double-leg takedown and proceeded to mount him and go to town furiously. This was definitely not my finest hour because the man ended up with a broken orbital socket and pursued litigation against me. I was exonerated from wrongdoing after a judge determined it to be self-defense. However, these types of incidents were beginning to occur more frequently. As a result, I quickly spiraled downward.

It was at this point I woke up in that bus station, bankrupt financially and emotionally. I was alone. The karma produced by my behavior had finally caught up with me. This was the defining moment when I realized something must change, as I was officially at rock bottom and financially bankrupt. In behavior analytic terms, this is called an *establishing operation*. It was this state of deprivation from my loved ones and being homeless that was the catalyst for desperate behavior change. This was the darkest moment of my life. My previous divorce left me half a million dollars in debt, most of which was not dischargeable in bankruptcy. This was also the moment that I realized that the science of behavior analysis that I practiced from nine to five on weekdays was my only option to pull myself out of this dark hole. I just needed to practice it during all waking hours seven days per week, and not just during my day job. I had to live and breathe these principles in my own life as well. It was this moment that I began to live and breathe the behavior analytic principles that underlie the following 5 life and leadership laws.

Pinpointing – Each morning, I pinpointed the results I was striving for and the behaviors that had the most impact on the achievement of these results. In my case, it was aspirations to see my daughter and family and achieve sobriety that drove me to putting my nose to the grindstone with my behavioral consultation business and exercise. After all, I knew an important behavioral science law, which was to decrease bad habits, I needed to increase appropriate alternative behaviors that served the same function.

Goal Setting – Every morning I woke up and looked at very carefully detailed pictures and written words that were measurable which were (1) my health and weight loss, (2) my family that I was unable to see due to court orders, (3) business results for our consultation group that served many vulnerable learners, (4) service to others without wanting anything in return, and (5) building the financial resources to pay off the half a million dollars in debt and get out of bankruptcy.

Self-Monitoring & Reporting Out Progress – At the end of every day, I rated my performance on the progress toward these goals using a behaviorally anchored rating scale (BARS). I journaled my progress toward each with great detail. One element to the self-monitoring, I must admit, that was only partially completed was reporting out my progress to someone to hold me accountable. In this case, I reported it to my matrimonial attorney and my beloved Marlene [my fiancé], whom I hoped would accept me back into her life.

Reciprocal Feedback – My report outs, although a little sporadic, were helpful because I received feedback from my attorney and Marlene, my fiancé. They both kept me motivated as they pointed out ways I could improve, and I responded in a reciprocal fashion to let them know how their feedback had helped me.

Pay For Performance – For most of these healthy productive behaviors that replaced my poor habits, financial payment was not the reinforcer with the exception of the business beginning to double in revenue each year, which allowed me to dig my way out of chapter 7 bankruptcy. The more meaningful pay-offs were that I was able to see my daughter again on a set weekly schedule that the courts agreed to. Another meaningful pay off was that Marlene began interacting with me again and showing she loved me. Fast-forwarding another eight years, and the business was exceeding eight-figure annual revenue and created over six hundred jobs across five states in the United States.

The final outcome, we now have one of the largest and most well-known behavior analytic organizations in the world serving the needs of vulnerable learners, their families, and the leaders and employees of struggling organizations. And most importantly, my daughter and Marlene have allowed me back into their lives. None of this would have occurred without harnessing behavioral karma through the power of the 5 laws of life and leadership.

So, what's the point of this story? Well, it doesn't matter whether you are trying to be more successful personally or professionally, the 5 laws of life and leadership can help you to get out of your deepest hole—and achieve your wildest dreams, as illustrated in this compelling real-life account.

While the above story might be described as serendipity, as behavioral scientists, we know there are clear behavioral principles at work through the 5 laws. Like capturing lightning in a bottle, understanding and applying these principles across life and leadership can help you behave in ways that accelerate productivity and lead to more meaningful and successful outcomes. And remember this as we move forward: Even if you don't have an official leadership position within an organization, you are still a leader in some capacity, especially because your day-to-day actions model what others will follow. After all, at a minimum, you are leading your own life. So, as we discuss leadership principles in the context of an organization or in any capacity, know that the principles still apply to everyone, everywhere, regardless of their title. This means behavioral karma is present everywhere in your life and the lives of others. Before we dive deep into the 5 laws, let's look at the ABC's of life and leadership through more of a scientific lens. We promise we will not remain too "sciencey" as the book goes on; however, we felt it important for you to have a fundamental understanding of many of the underlying principles behind leading a life or leading within an organization that is the foundation of this book.

The journey of leadership starts with understanding your personal story. Not just about reflecting on your experiences but digging deeper into the impact of those experiences on you, and the impact of what you said and did on those with whom you were a part of their personal experience! When it comes to leading, it's not just about you. This was a hard lesson we had to learn earlier in life. Many leaders tend to judge themselves by their intentions. And in everyday life, most people do as well. The reality is, others are not judging you by your intention, but by your impact. Your behavior has the potential to be highly contagious, and the behavior of those around you may be a symptom of your leadership. And like karma, the impact of your behavior on and across others has the ability to directly affect you, as you are paired with something good or something bad. We've witnessed this firsthand on many occasions. If you are an organizational leader, manager, school leader, classroom leader, team leader, line leader, athletic leader, household leader, or anybody who has the potential to influence an individual or group of people, take a look at the behavior of those around you. How do they behave in your presence? What do they say? Are they happy? Do they laugh? Do they seek you out and ask for your advice? Do they admit when they made a mistake? Do they volunteer for projects? Do they share creative ideas? Do they speak up at training? Do they follow through when you ask them to do something? Or do they become silent in your presence? Avoid you? Deny mistakes and blame others? Frequently call in sick? Remain silent in your presence? Look unhappy? These reactions may be a measure of your leadership. Would you want to be led by you?

Like the proverbial pebble, your behavior has the power to have a ripple effect that impacts every facet of relationships, families, schools, teams, and organizations. And the consequences that your behavior has on your environment, in turn, directly impact you. This is behavioral karma. If this consequence is valued, the behavior of those around you will likely occur again and might be thought of as positive behavioral karma. For example, if you teach an employee how to do something that produces an improved outcome, and in turn, they teach their peers and this produces multiple improved outcomes, this might be thought of as positive behavioral karma. If this consequence is not valued or even aversive, those around you will do just enough to avoid the consequence, and this might be thought of as negative behavioral karma. For example, if you yell at your spouse, they may, in turn, yell at your children, who, in turn, may perform poorly at school that day and misbehave in class. Then, the next thing you know, the teacher is requesting you to come in for a parent meeting to discuss your child's behavior. This isn't good! And because the behaviors of people are often interlocking, you might experience instant behavioral karma. For example, if you smile at somebody, the person you smile at might smile back. You, in turn, might smile at other people throughout the day, and so might they. Then those people smile at others, and the ripple effect of positive and instant behavioral karma continues. And of course, there is delayed behavioral karma as we don't always experience the direct impact of our behavior. For example, if you help somebody now, they may help you later. Or in the example above, if you are regularly smiling and treating people kindly within your organization, it has the potential to progressively boost morale, retention, and performance as multiple employees reproduce the behavior in the form of regularly smiling and treating others with kindness. These are all delayed but positive outcomes of your behavior.

In failing organizations and failing families, oftentimes the focus is solely on the use of authority to manage behavior through accountability measures. "You'd better get this done or else" is the never-ending mantra of the day. This approach likely produces negative behavioral karma because people tend to feel unsafe. Like the boss who hammers their employees for coming in a little bit late on a few occasions, but fails to recognize all of the extra time they put in after hours. As a result, productivity, innovation, and morale are squashed as people, whether they are your employees, family members, or peers, will do just enough to get by. In the example above, employees might end up coming to work on time every day, but they stop putting in extra time, thought, or passion into their projects. However, in the most productive and sustained organizations, teams, groups, families, etc., people feel inspired and hold themselves responsible for their behavior and outcomes (Geller, 2003). In fact, in the case of excellent organizations, leaders frequently hold themselves accountable for their followers' behaviors and even take ownership of other people's mistakes. The same goes for families. If a child is misbehaving or not performing well, the parent will reflect on their own behavior to think about how they better support their child. These leaders (including household leaders!) know their followers' behavior is directly influenced by the environment they've engineered for them. Good household leaders know that the most important part of their family unit is their children, and they treat them as such. Similarly, good organizational leaders recognize that employees are the most valuable part of the organization, and they are treated as such. This is often evident in sports organizations where players' physical, nutritional, psychological, safety, and educational needs are a priority. The never-ending mantra of the day in these types of organizations is, "I can't wait to get this done to see the outcome." Why? Because they likely feel cared for, safe, and satisfied with their position. Under these conditions, folks can be found daily going above and beyond; moreover, innovation and morale are abundant. This is a result of great leaders who focus on creating a safe environment that taps into people's talents and collectively engages them toward shared accomplishment. Whether it's a child stepping out of their comfort zone to speak in front of the class as a result of the teacher's classroom leadership, or an employee stepping up with a new innovation, great leaders regardless of context know that fostering a safe environment results in fearless tenacity and innovation without negative consequences for small failures. It allows for people to push the envelope to success.

Safety is extremely important for achieving success—especially psychological safety. We will talk more about the power of psychological safety as a means of achieving success in a later chapter. But for now, what's important to understand is that success is the result of behavior. Period, end of story. No successful result can be achieved without behavior. It's not luck, not genetics, not money, and not personality. It's simply behavior! Oh, and by the way, for those of you who wish you had those charismatic personality traits of your favorite actor, actress, or whoever, know this: When anybody talks about personality, what they are talking about is behavior. Their personality is made up of a bunch of micro-behaviors if you will. When these behaviors occur regularly and are attributed to an individual, we say it's their personality. The same goes for other adjectives like character, nature, disposition, persona, temperament, and so on. It's all behavior. And at the root of each of these behaviors are the same behavioral principles embedded in the 5 laws that we will outline in this book. It doesn't matter what you want to do or what you want to help others do. These behavioral principles can help you better plan for and engage in the appropriate actions to help you or others achieve valued outcomes and be successful in any area. For example, if you are interested in crochet (hey, don't knock it until you've tried it!), you can apply the principles of behavior to help both yourself and others become the best crocheters around. It may sound funny, but it's true. And if you are like us and interested in making a positive dent in the world, well, understanding the principles of behavior will be critical to your success, given that many of the world's problems are a direct result of human behavior. It doesn't matter if you are interested in sports, education, politics, engineering, construction, medicine, hospitality, culinary arts, or communications, or perhaps you just want to be the best parent or partner you can be. Understanding these principles, along with practical applications, will allow you to be more effective in reaching your goals or supporting others while achieving success in any field or aspect of life. The information in this book will be life-changing.

KEY TAKEAWAYS:

- » The 5 laws can be used to get you out of the darkest of personal and professional holes.
- » The 5 laws provide a framework for accelerating productivity and achieving meaningful outcomes.
- » Success is the result of behavior.
- » Your behavior impacts the behavior of others.
- » The behavior of others impacts you.

ASK YOURSELF:

- » Are you truly aware of the impact of your behavior on people? How do you know?
- » Are you aware of the impact of other people's behavior on you? How do you know?
- » Does this awareness include the impact on thoughts, feelings, and actions?

CHAPTER 3

The Scientific ABCs of Life and Leadership

As you may have noticed, the title of our book includes the word leadership. Leadership is important in almost every area of your life – personally and professionally. This is why we are choosing to explore leadership further before unpacking the 5 laws as they are inextricably related. Fundamentally, leadership is about behavior, your behavior, and the behavior of others. Since we are talking about behavior, what better lens to explore it through than the science of human behavior to understand it at a deeper level. Within the science, the *antecedent, behavior, consequence model (ABC model)* or three-term contingency is as important in the explanation to the nature of human behavior and leadership as $E=MC^2$ is to explain the nature of energy. Excuse us while we get "sciencey" again. We promise it won't last long, and while everything discussed throughout the book is rooted in the science of human behavior, we won't dive this deep into it again in future chapters. However, we do want you to understand that we aren't making this stuff up and it's not a flavor of the month approach to achieving success. We also want you to have a working knowledge of what's driving your behavior and the behavior of others, as this is fundamental to deliberately generating lots of positive behavioral karma!

A Peek at Behavior through a Scientific Lens

Technically speaking, antecedents of behavior are stimulus events, situations, or circumstances that precede an operant response (Miltenberger, 2004), which is just a fancy word for behavior. In layman's terms, antecedents are things that come before behavior (the operant response as we just noted) and essentially tell it what to do; however, both positive and negative consequences maintain behavior and potentially create conditions where people are going to go above and beyond. More on positive and negative consequences in a moment as it probably ain't whacha think! Unfortunately, while most leaders and managers in organizations attempt to achieve success by focusing on antecedents like training, goal setting, and giving directives because it gets behavior going, it is consequences that are key to increasing and sustaining productive staff performance. If setting goals and telling people what to do resulted in peak performance and achievement of objectives, most people and organizations would be highly successful. And this goes for you as a leader and manager of your own life as it is what happens as a result of your behavior that increases the likelihood you will continue it. More on that shortly, but let's just dive a little deeper into the science, so you get the full picture of why behavior happens and leverage this knowledge to improve your own habits, and perhaps the habits of others.

Now to many, consequences are perceived as something bad that happens following misbehavior or bad performance. And this is true, sometimes. Consequences or *postcedents*, from a behaviorist's perspective, are simply things that happen as a result of a behavior and make it more or less likely that a given behavior will occur. There's about a century's worth of research that confirms that a significant proportion of behaviors are maintained by consequences, or what we commonly refer to as a *function*. Consider the young child crying. The behavior of crying allows the child access to meaningful consequences. For example, perhaps the child is provided food or her mother's attention. When the child receives food or attention, the behavior of crying leads to a meaningful consequence, which increases the likelihood the child will cry again in order to access the food or attention. In other cases, the child may cry because her diaper is dirty. In this case, the meaningful consequence becomes the removal of the dirty diaper. The antecedent of a dirty diaper evokes the behavior of crying, which then results in something that doesn't feel good, or what we refer to as an aversive, being removed. Make sense? Placing these examples into the ABC formula (fig. 1):

ABC Formula	Something Added (R+)	Something Subtracted (R-)
Antecedent	Child wants attention	Child is uncomfortable because of a dirty diaper
Behavior	Child cries	Child cries
Consequence	Mother adds attention	Mother subtracts dirty diaper

Figure 1: Examples of ABC formula

Simply put, behavior often occurs as a result of getting something, which is known in science as *positive reinforcement* or getting rid of something, which is known in science as negative reinforcement. Many folks are often confused by the concepts of *positive* and *negative reinforcement*, as the words positive and negative are associated with good or bad. In actuality, as behavioral scientists view it in regard to human behavior, positive simply means something is added as a result of behavior, and negative means something is subtracted, as in the illustrations above. These "somethings" can be related to accessing or escaping persons, places, things, and even private events like thoughts, feelings, and other sensations within the body.

To be successful, we all must learn complex chains of behaviors that allow us to get our needs met. But we all start with the smallest steps. For example, as a young child, we might point to a favorite toy and say "toy" if we want it. Eventually, we are taught to string words together to make sentences and sentences together to hold a conversation. It's not long before we are reading and writing, and then using those skills to work our way through school. As we progress through life, we learn to engage in a bunch of other behaviors that are chained together and eventually allow us to achieve meaningful outcomes across different conditions. Like learning to drive, a complex set of behaviors, if broken down, allows many of us to access a variety of important things in our personal and professional lives.

And sometimes, we behave in certain ways because the resulting consequences make us feel good or feel better. For instance, most people help others because they've learned that helping others is good, and therefore helping behaviors often provide positive reinforcement in the form of social attention, which gives us a good feeling. They aren't necessarily getting something, like a tangible or praise, but they do it because they've learned to value helping others as a result of their history of positive reinforcement for engaging in helping behavior; therefore, the act of helping others produces positive reinforcement in the form of a good feeling.

For example, we were once giving a speech related to leadership and the principles of behavior. Somebody raised their hand and referred to the incident that happened on the 9/11 attacks and said, "So you are going to tell me that those first responders rushed into burning buildings because they thought they were going to get something for it?" Our answer was, "Of course not!" In this case and many others, people rushed in because they *valued* helping others. That was likely the reinforcement. Doing good for others is like instant behavioral karma for those of us who enjoy helping. It makes us feel good to help. If every person and leader valued helping others the way those first responders did, our world would be a different place. But to bring it back to the science, when we refer to values, we are referring to what is reinforcing to an individual, as evidenced by their behavior increasing. Not what they say, what they do. Let's continue to discover why behavior happens – and continues to happen.

Events and Rules

While the above describes what behavioral scientists call contingency shaped or event-governed behaviors that occur because they come in direct contact with consequences, there are also behaviors that occur because they are rule-governed. In other words, sometimes we don't experience things directly, but we behave in ways as a result of our understanding of rules and consequences as they are described to us. It be might be better understood as "verbally governed" (Vargas, 1988) as it is influenced by verbal antecedents, such as somebody giving you instructions (e.g., a husband picks up his clothes because his wife tells him to) or reacting to one's own private thinking (e.g., a person starts an exercise program after thinking, "I'm overweight"). We will discuss rule-governed behavior in a later chapter.

For now, the biggest difference between rule-governed and event-governed behavior is knowledge of consequences versus direct contact to consequences. To understand the rules, we must have been taught them, remember them, and then learned the right time to apply them. For instance, when you were a child, your mom or dad may have warned you to never put a knife in the toaster if the toast got stuck. In contrast, event-governed behavior is contingent. In other words, people behave in certain ways because their actions are directly exposed to consequences. For example, you put a knife in the toaster, and you received a shock. As a result, you no longer put knives in the toaster. We were clearly not the sharpest knives in the drawer as we were both warned by our parents not put the knife in the toaster, but we did it anyway, got shocked, and then we both did it again down the road. Don't laugh at us. But please join in and laugh *with us*! We were ridiculous. But the science can actually explain our repeated behavior in that the initial consequence (the shock) wasn't intense enough to sufficiently punish our foolish behavior!

We will touch on rule-governed behavior a little bit more in the next chapter. But for now, what's important to know is that whether rule or event governed, in most cases, our behaviors are actually impacted by a variety of potential reinforcers. For example, most folks work in education to access multiple positive reinforcers like helping students achieve, socially interacting with peers, and obtaining a paycheck. At the same time, potential aversives (i.e., things we prefer to avoid), like late payments, bill collectors calling, or being evicted, are avoided!

In the end, accomplishing valued outcomes can be broken down into behavior. All results require somebody doing something more, less, or differently, a fact that we will reflect on throughout this book. So, if we want to achieve results, we must improve our behavior.

And if we want to improve behavior, it makes sense to look at it through the ABC lens rooted in the *science* of human behavior. We will dive deeper into the concept in the pay for performance chapter. But let's further explore concepts related to leading and managing. Whether personally or professionally, these concepts are important if you truly wish to make a difference in your life or the lives of others. Now let's get back to leadership.

Is It Better to Lead or Manage? (Yourself and Others)

Now that we have that out of the way let's investigate leadership. Now. if you are not in a formal leadership or management position, you might be thinking, "what the hell does this have to do with me or behavioral karma?" Well, here are a couple of things to consider. First, if you aren't in a formal leadership or management position and you are working in an organization, you are likely to be led or managed. But even if you aren't, you might still be leading or managing from your current position, or perhaps you are a parent leading and managing a household. And if you aren't a parent, you are at least leading a life and managing your own behavior and affairs at some level. So, these concepts are important for everybody to understand at some level as everybody is leading and managing in one more aspect of their lives.

According to a 2014 study by the Center for Creative Leadership, close to 40 percent of new chief executives are not successful within their first eighteen months on the job, and most fail to live up to the expectations established by the company. This, as suggested by Hewerston (2014), is likely because the expected behaviors and actions related to the leadership role have not been clearly defined. We find this unfortunate, as we don't think it's a stretch to say that people need to understand the contextual expectations of an organization if they are to effectively lead and manage under varying conditions. While we touched on leadership and management a bit earlier, let's dig into this topic a little bit more.

The term leadership is frequently used in literature and across organizations, but the definition is often imprecise. Among other things, it's been described as a trait, ability, skill, and relationship reflected through styles of leadership like *transformational, democratic, authoritarian,* and *laissez-faire* (Northouse, 2015). This makes leadership development challenging given there is no singular set of competencies applicable across situations. Researcher and author Dr. Peter Northouse (2007) suggests that leadership is "a process whereby an individual influences a group of individuals to achieve a common goal." He has found upward of seventy different classification systems of leadership, many of which have evolved over the last few decades.

But regardless of the topography (the way it looks) or style of leadership, the prevailing thought is that the function of leadership is to influence people (well, influence behavior, from our perspective) toward a common goal. Older perspectives regarding leadership hold that power which comes from the position on the organizational chart, leaders should rule, and the measure of the leader can be found in the bottom line. In contrast, more modern and humanitarian views on leadership rooted in the science of human behavior suggest that an organizational chart is just a management tool, not a leadership locator, and power comes from the people as manifested in their behavior (Daniels & Daniels, 2007). Unfortunately, too many leaders make the mistake of leading by results. The problem with this approach is that results can often be obtained through a variety of ways, including those that are unethical. For example, places like Wells Fargo thought the ends justified the means when they unethically led their managers into creating fake accounts to meet performance expectations. While the numbers or results initially told one story, the behaviors told another story as there were numerous legal, ethical, management, and social responsibility transgressions (Cavico & Mutjaba, 2017). This is why it's important to have a clear understanding of the behaviors that lead to specific results. Since behavior is countable, measuring leadership provides an opportunity to collect cold hard data related to leadership (as opposed to judgment). Dr. Aubrey Daniels, the father of organizational behavior management or the science of human behavior as applied to the workplace, suggests the following as leadership metrics (2007):

- **Mass** – Number of followers responding to the leader
- **Velocity** – Amount of time it takes for followers to respond
- **Direction** – Number of followers moving toward the goal
- **Vision** – Number of followers maintaining a clear focus on vision over time
- **Values** – Number of followers performing ethically
- **Persistence** – Number of followers putting forth continuous effort toward goals
- **Teamwork** – Frequency of cooperation among followers
- **Trust** – Number of followers willing to admit mistakes
- **Respect** – Number of followers reinforcing rather than punishing

> **LEADERSHIP IS LIFTING A PERSON'S VISION TO HIGH SIGHTS, THE RAISING OF A PERSON'S PERFORMANCE. TO A HIGHER STANDARD, THE BUILDING OF A PERSONALITY BEYOND ITS NORMAL LIMITATIONS.**
>
> *- Peter Drucker*

If you noticed, this approach to measuring leadership is likely different from others you've heard of because it makes everything empirical as it is countable in terms of frequency or duration. This can be an extremely powerful tool for becoming an objective observer of the impact of leadership, including the impact of your own leadership. As Dr. Daniels reminds us, "The intentional search for the impact of your actions sets you apart from those who try to replicate the actions of other leaders" (2007).

There are also some folks who confuse leadership with management, think one is better than the other or think they are one and the same. But there is a difference. And like the quarterback and the wide receiver, leadership and management are complementary and typically both required for the regular pursuit and accomplishment of short- and long-term goals. Researcher and author Dr. Scott Geller succinctly discriminates between the two when he writes, "Simply put, managers hold people accountable, whereas leaders inspire people to feel responsible" (2003).

You see, effective leaders focus on strengthening relationships, facilitating self-accountability, and using feedback to make progress toward goal attainment a source of value and reinforcement (Daniels, 2000). And effective managers facilitate order, consistency, and accountability using performance feedback to let people know where they stand in relation to goals, and what should be done to move closer to them (Balacazar, Hopkins, & Suarez, 1986). And effective leaders and managers foster effective self-management to foster independence and help employees take better responsibility to achieve desired outcomes through the regular monitoring, recording, and rewarding their own behavior (Godat & Brigham, 1999). That makes sense through a professional lens. But let's take a look at it in a couple of examples through a personal lens. For example, if you are a parent who is effectively leading a household with young children, this means you serve as a source of encouragement who likely focuses on your family members communicating well and pursuing meaningful outcomes related to areas like school and personal interests. And if you are a parent who is also managing well, you likely ensure your children do their homework, brush their teeth, take a bath, clean their rooms, and follow through with routines that allow for the maintenance of a clean and organized household that aligns with your values and standards. And you are likely teaching them self-management skills as they ask themselves questions like "Did I do my chores," or "Am I caught up with all of my schoolwork?" If you are living solo, you might be leading your own life by pursuing your niche or allowing your vision to influence your actions in that direction. And if you are managing or self-managing your life, you are probably paying bills, organizing your schedule, and working through your own problems. And, of course, these concepts can be applied to other personal examples like living with a friend, a significant other, or perhaps a roommate in college. In any case, you may engage in leading, managing, or both.

While not a precise description of leadership and management behavior, Kotter (1990) differentiates between the two through these basic functions (fig. 2):

MANAGEMENT Produce Order & Consistency	LEADERSHIP Produces Change & Movement
Planning and Budgeting	Establishing Direction
Organizing and Staffing	Aligning People
Controlling and Problem Solving	Motivating and Inspiring

Figure 2: Management vs. Leadership Functions

Many people get caught up on the title of leader or manager. People can lead or manage from any place. Regardless of their position or status, everyone in almost any situation has an opportunity to help manage situations and influence others in a way that makes a positive difference. Sometimes leaders must manage, and at other times, managers must lead. Where leaders outline a path and get people to move collectively in the right direction, managers coordinate and ensure folks stay on course. In fact, Daniels & Daniels (2007) suggest that the durability of the leader's vision is dependent on the quality of management and therefore needs to be involved in management as much as necessary to ensure systems and processes are in place. At times this may require managing the managers. In many cases, whether it's personally and professionally, it's not unusual for you to lead, manage, and at the same time, be led and managed. We can't emphasize this enough. Leading and managing is not about the title. It's about function. Remember what Geller (2003) boiled it down to: leadership is about inspiration, and management is about accountability. So, it doesn't matter what position you hold in a company, team, peer group, within your household, etc. If you are inspiring people, you are likely to lead. If you are holding people accountable, you are likely managing.

> A GOOD MANAGER FINDS SATISFACTION IN HELPING OTHERS BE PRODUCTIVE, NOT BEING THE MOST PRODUCTIVE PERSON IN THE ROOM.
>
> *- Paul Glen*

When it comes to being successful in your personal life, it's easy to see how leading and managing are important for achieving desired outcomes. Like successful leaders, those who lead a successful life create a vision of where they want to be one day, outline a path toward that vision, and then consistently manage their behavior to stay on track. They become experts in accomplishing goals, and along the way, they generate heaps of positive behavioral karma. But what is an expert, and how do you become one? Let's dive into that in the next chapter on experts and just touch a little bit more on some of the scientific underpinnings.

KEY TAKEAWAYS:

   » Antecedents function to get behavior going.
   » Consequences function to keep behavior.
   » Most behavior continues to occur because of what happens as a result of it.
   » Some behavior occurs because of "rules" that have been taught to us.

- » Leadership isn't about the title; it's about inspiration and influencing yourself and others.
- » The measure of a leader can be found in the behavior of the followers.
- » Managing is about accountability; whether it be areas related to self-management or managing others.

ASK YOURSELF:

- » What are some regular behaviors you engage in personally and professionally?
- » What happens as a result of those behaviors?
- » Are the outcomes meaningful to you?
- » Under what conditions (antecedents) are you most likely to engage in those behaviors?
- » What areas of your life are you leading either personally or professionally?
- » What areas of your life are you managing either personally or professionally?
- » Based on what you've learned about leadership, how are the "leaders" you've observed matching up to the leadership metrics identified by Daniels (2007)?

CHAPTER 4

Experts in Leadership and Life Aren't Born, They Are Made

Many people believe the best of the best are born, not made. However, we subscribe to the experts-are-made model of leadership development because it's too difficult to discount the concepts of hard work, dedication, devotion, commitment and all the other qualifiers that those who lead a quality organization or quality life put into their development to become the best they can. Remember, this means being someone who can bring out the best in others and yourself. Of course, we don't dismiss the concept of natural talent (genetic predisposition), but you can't control that aspect. What you can control is the quantity and quality of the learning you participate in, as well as the quantity and quality of the behaviors you engage in. The best way to improve the quantity and quality of your leadership is to integrate effective strategies into your daily leadership behaviors that have been developed and refined through years of practice and research. In short, create good leadership habits. But sometimes, this is easier said than done.

Build This and It Will Come

Unfortunately, when happiness and success are hard to find in one's life or profession, the typical fix is for somebody, somewhere (sometimes it's self-talk!) to say, "You need to get your $h!t together." If this worked, many of society's ailments would be erased, as the phrase, or one with similar intent regularly bounces off household and organizational walls across the continent. In leadership and everyday life, happiness and success occur as the result of behavior. Not talent, not personality, but the behavior that makes up these adjectives. That is, folks must do something more, less, or differently if they are to achieve happiness or success. Once you understand your values, the achievement of goals will only occur through sustainable and productive behavior. This includes your personal behavior and in the case of organizational leadership, the behavior of followers as you seek to help yourself and others develop the ability to do the right thing in the right way across varied situations. When these behaviors occur consistently and automatically, they are often referred to by behavior analysts as *habit strength behaviors*. Or in short, habits. When most people talk about habits, they are usually referring to bad habits. But what they are talking about is developing good or productive habits. Creating productive habits requires shaping or the reinforcement of successive approximations toward desired performance goals. Like the sculptor slowly molding her art toward a vision in mind, shaping progressively builds behavior toward a performance goal. Once a behavior is developed and successfully repeated, fluency occurs as evidenced by a performance that occurs at a rapid rate and is precise, durable, and automatic. Like the boxer who regularly and successively slips a punch, this type of performance occurs quickly and without thinking. In short, it's a really good habit!

> WE ARE WHAT WE REPEATEDLY DO. EXCELLENCE, THEN, IS NOT AN ACT, BUT A HABIT.
>
> **- Aristotle**

And we can't say this enough. In fact, we'll keep saying it. In life or leadership, it is your responsibility to create opportunities for yourself or the people you lead to practice critical behaviors correctly, deliver or seek out regular feedback, and get yourself and others in contact with meaningful outcomes. When people behave in ways that lead them toward who and what they value, the behaviors that lead them in that direction are likely to occur again and accelerate the achievement of success. More on this later.

Small Steps to Achieve Big Change

As the old saying goes, "If everything is important, nothing is important." Therefore, it's vital to point out that you don't need to focus on changing every behavior at once. That is, your behavior or the behavior of others. This is a big mistake people make personally and professionally. Most think that focusing on only a few behaviors is unreasonable as it delays the achievement of important goals when "there's a lot to do!" We will dive deeper into this in our chapter on pinpointing. But for now, it's important to understand that science of human behavior has demonstrated this: Whether your behavior or the behavior of others, focusing on shaping only a few critical behaviors aligned with desired results actually accelerates performance and attainment of goals. Try it yourself. The next time you come across an important concept or skill that you want to learn, how will you go about learning it? Will you read the entire book and expect that all knowledge and skills will be at your disposal? Or do you need to break down the sections, read them again, and perhaps think about how a concept might apply to your life? When you've successfully created a productive habit, were you focusing on changing many habits, or just one or two at a time? Or consider teaching a child to read. They aren't given an entire paragraph and then taught that way. They are first taught the alphabet, then a small word, and then the words are strung together to teach a sentence, the sentences strung together to make a paragraph. Whether children or adults, this is the way we learn. The big benefit of being an adult is that new knowledge and skills can be built upon prior knowledge and skills. So if you want to become an expert leader of your own life or positively influence others to achieve big things, don't try to do everything at once. Rather, focus on building just a couple of critical habits at a time: your habits and the habits of others.

Experts in Life and Leadership Are Developed Through Repetition

A quick note on experts: the conceptual definition of an *expert* in the scientific literature is not as consistent as one may think (Edmonds & Gavoni, 2017). The general definition of an expert is "an individual who can perform a particular task at a high level on a consistent basis." But then, what is a "high level"? The bottom line is an expert is someone who possesses the ability to perform at a level where others cannot, or only a few can. The definition is not exact, and it never will be. The amount of time it takes to become an expert is not exact, and it never will be either. To emphasize the point, you can imagine that not all great leaders develop at the same rate under the same conditions.

> THE MAN WHO MOVES A MOUNTAIN BEGINS BY CARRYING
> AWAY SMALL STONES.
>
> ### *- Confucius*

With that said, if you want to accelerate critical leadership habits (e.g., delivering effective feedback), you must engage in deliberate practice. This first requires an understanding of what deliberate practice is and then transforming current practice or training into deliberate practice. The simple fact is that the primary mechanism that separates non-experts and experts is the amount of deliberate practice one has engaged in over the years.

Deliberate practice can be employed, for example, by taking a critical leadership behavior like delivering feedback and breaking it down into all its components and understanding all aspects of it. Next, it requires practicing the application of the behavior across scenarios related to executing each component that leads up to the delivery of feedback and then practicing it repeatedly until proficiency is achieved. To accelerate the achievement of proficiency, it's always helpful to have a coach. This doesn't have to be a formal coach, but perhaps somebody that can give you feedback. In the case of this example, feedback on your feedback!

Study Exemplars and Non-Exemplars

We will explore the benefits of self-monitoring in regard to personal and large-scale organizational performance improvement in a future chapter. But for now, think of self-monitoring as you just being a better observer of your habits. Similarly, you can also observe the habits of others, as observational learning can accelerate your development of habits. One can actually learn a new skill by watching others and copying their habits. For example, we love Simon Sinek and have watched many of his TedTalks, as he has discussed and modeled for us certain aspects of leadership. As former athletes, we watched videos all of the time to better learn techniques from professionals who were teaching and modeling it. This type of video modeling is easier to access than ever before, as anyone can effortlessly find several clips of experts talking about and demonstrating leadership behavior. After studying these films, a simple behavior hack would be setting up a camera and recording yourself attempting a particular leadership strategy. This video feedback can be a powerful tool for helping you recognize what you are doing well and where you might have opportunities for improvement. Or, if you manage a team or lead in an organization, record your meetings. After you have recorded yourself, compare your performance to the experts. Was it similar? What was missing? Make a note of what is good and what needs to be improved, and if you are leading a meeting, also make a note of how others responded to you. This is all very useful data. You can also request other experts to review it to provide you feedback or compare notes as a form of interobserver agreement. In other words, are you both seeing the same thing? Beyond just studying others, good leaders must observe the conditions under which they were most successful and try to discriminate what they did that led to that success.

> WE CANNOT CHANGE WHAT WE ARE NOT AWARE OF, AND ONCE WE ARE AWARE, WE CANNOT HELP BUT CHANGE.
>
> *- Sheryl Sandberg*

Many folks think they can only learn from gurus or successful people. However, we contend that learning can occur by observing anyone around you. When you become a good observer of behavior and the impact of behavior on the environment (remember, people are part of the environment), your mind begins processing the numerous bits of data that are garnered from the series of contingencies or if-thens observed on a daily basis. This allows us to form rules or verbal descriptions that let us know performing certain behaviors within a given setting will result in a particular outcome (Tarbox, Zuckerman, Bishop, Olive, & O'Hora, 2011). You remember, this is what we described as rule-governed behavior. While you've never experienced that outcome or the contingencies the rule describes, you understand, "If I do X, then Y will occur" (Skinner, 1974). As a result, you behave according to the rule. For example, "If you run through a red light, then you may get into a car accident or receive a ticket." While you may never have been in a car accident, you will likely behave according to the rule. In this case, to avoid the undesirable outcome of getting into a car accident or receiving a ticket, you behave accordingly.

There is a lot to be learned by connecting behavior with results. Whether it's your behavior or the behavior of others. Though it's not the only solution for becoming a better leader, understanding behavior allows for the prediction of an outcome, thus increasing the likelihood you will respond or behave in the right way and improve your chances of success. And this includes responding appropriately and consistently to achieve meaningful outcomes, even in the presence of adversity. What some people know as grit. Since achieving meaningful outcomes usually requires people to overcome obstacles and produce positive behavioral karma, let's further explore the concept of grit through a behavioral lens.

Developing Grit to Achieve Success

Cus D'Amato, famed boxing trainer of Mike Tyson, once said, "When two men are fighting, what you're watching is more a contest of wills than of skills, with the stronger, will usually overcoming the skill. The skill will prevail only when it is so superior to the other man's skill that the will is not tested." This statement reminds us of the concept known as *grit*. While around for decades and used interchangeably with adjectives like *toughness* and *backbone*, grit has received lots of attention since Angela Duckworth's TED Talk on the topic. But what is grit? Will it help you to achieve short- and long-term goals? Where can one find it? Can it be purchased? Is it a trait people are born with? If you take one "grit" each day, will you become grittier? Or if you repeat to yourself daily, "I think I can, I think I can," will that make you gritty? Can tell yourself or others to be grittier make it happen?

What the Hell Is Grit?

ADVERSITY CAUSES SOME MEN TO BREAK;
OTHERS TO BREAK RECORDS.

- William Arthur Ward

Many dictionaries use verbiage like courage, resolve, and strength of character to define grit. In the *Journal of Personality and Social Psychology*, Duckworth (2007) defined grit as "perseverance and passion toward long-term goals." While this makes good sense, we do not believe it quite captures the scope of grit. Now, excuse us again, but we are going to need to get a little bit "sciency" again for just a few paragraphs. The concept of grit may need to be redefined, and the foundation examined through a conceptual lens employed by behavioral scientists such as B. F. Skinner and Albert Bandura. From a radical behaviorist's perspective (i.e., Skinner's), grit might simply mean choosing a larger delayed consequence over a smaller more immediate one as it applies to short- and long-term goals, or what is more commonly known as *self-control* (Lerman, Addison, & Kodak, 2006). Over time, and as a result of regular and successful performance and goal achievement, one develops what Bandura (1997) calls *self-efficacy*, or one's belief in their ability to complete a given task.

Now, the hardcore behavior analyst might suggest self-efficacy is the result of "contingencies of reinforcement that establish a correspondence between such verbal predictions and the behavior to which they refer" (Biglan, 1987). But we doubt you, as the reader, are concerned with the theoretical underpinnings. What's important to know is that this reported belief has been found to be a large predictor of success and the likelihood that an individual will continue to pursue goals (i.e., demonstrate self-control). It could also be perceived by behavioral scientists as resistance to extinction or behaving under conditions where there is little to no reinforcement available. In the end, grit might simply be considered a more attractive word that embodies concepts related to self-control or self-efficacy. After all, there is a certain je ne sais quoi when a person is referred to as being gritty as opposed to somebody who possesses self-control, self-efficacy or resistance to extinction (i.e., a behavior goes away because it has not been reinforced).

Why is this important? Well, you might look at somebody else and think, "Wow, they are tough. I wish I could hang in there like that!" Or "They are really able to persevere. I'd never been able to overcome those challenges to achieve what they did." Well, you can. They were not born that way. Their experiences increased their ability to maintain their behavior under challenging conditions. And the 5 laws, as outlined in this book, will provide you the tools for improving your ability to develop grit and achieve meaningful outcomes, regardless of the challenges presented.

By the way, as self-proclaimed behavioral ambassadors, we would be remiss if we didn't give you a little more insight on radical behaviorism, a philosophy of the science of behavior that has been widely misunderstood. Where earlier forms of behaviorism focused solely on overt behavior (i.e., what other people can see and hear you doing), Skinner put forth that radical behaviorism is a natural science, one that also seeks to explain private events or covert behavior that only you can observe, like your thoughts and feelings. At the time, this truly was a radical philosophy as compared with methodological behaviorism, the prevailing behaviorist philosophy of the time that acknowledged private events but did not consider them part of the science of behavior. We will be digging more into private events and how they impact behavior in later chapters. For now, what's important to know is that the science of human behavior *does* address thoughts and feelings, and both Skinner's and Bandura's work have been available for decades.

While terminology put forth by the science of human behavior might not sound as provocative as grit, understanding well-researched concepts such as goal setting and self-control will put you and others on the fast track to overcoming inner and outer adversity, achieving value-driven goals, and producing lots of positive behavioral karma under any conditions. In the next chapter, we will begin diving into the 5 laws, beginning with pinpointing.

KEY TAKEAWAYS:

- » Leaders are not born, they are developed through experience.
- » Good leadership is built on habits.
- » Working on just a couple of habits at a time will accelerate learning and achievement of goals.
- » We are not born with grit, it is developed through experience.
- » The science of human behavior addresses thoughts and feelings.

ASK YOURSELF:

- » Do you have thoughts and feelings show up that lead you to believe that you don't have what it takes to achieve something?
- » Have you identified an expert that you can seek out videos and articles to learn from?
- » Is there somebody around you that engages in certain productive habits that you can observe and learn from?
- » Have you identified habits you would like to build or change?
- » Are you only focusing on building one or two habits at a time?
- » Are you deliberately practicing in order to build your habit?

SECTION II

The 5 Laws

CHAPTER 5

Pinpointing

Oftentimes people fail to reach success because of faulty pinpointing. Given the importance of it, you would think everybody would know exactly what that is. Well, fear not! In this chapter, we will dive into the first of the 5 laws to share exactly what pinpointing is, help you understand exactly why pinpointing is so important, and show you how you can use pinpointing to achieve success across life in leadership. But first, let's dive into a quick story to illustrate how focusing or "pinpointing" just a couple of pivotal behaviors can create powerful positive behavioral karma that has a ripple effect across an entire organization.

Your Behavior Is Contagious – Paulie's Story

A long time ago, in a galaxy far, far away (well, actually it was only Florida), as a behavior analyst for a school district, I was unexpectedly thrown into my first turnaround (failing) school with some other folks to help get behavior under control and improve academic achievement. One day, I went into the school, a little bit tired, and a lot bit unmotivated. The fact was, I didn't feel good, and this was exacerbated by the intensity that comes from the daily grind of turning around and failing in school—especially a school that has high discipline issues.

As a newcomer to the school, I was shocked at the number of students I witnessed running down the hallways .3as they ignored staff's feeble attempts to get them to walk as they pushed, taunted, and yelled their way to their morning class. I also observed the teachers, heads hung low, facial expressions suggesting concern and exhaustion. They appeared defeated. Even in Leadership as well. Honestly, I had no idea what to do or where to begin. As a behavior analyst, I was trained in a single subject design methodology where I typically focused on supporting the behavior improvement of *one* individual, not in organizational behavior management (OBM), as I now am, where approaches focus on behavior and performance improvement of many.

One morning, as I slowly moped my way to my duty post to assist students with safely transitioning into the school, a little girl came up to me and handed me a flower. At that moment, I was immediately uplifted by the random act of kindness this first-grader decided to bestow upon me. I smiled, gratefully, and told her what a special little girl I thought she was. From that day forward, each time I saw the little girl, the large smile that crept across my face was quickly rewarded by the broad grin on the little girl's. In fact, because of my positive reaction to the student, other students began going out of their way to stop by and shyly wave and show their pearly whites as they smiled then deliberately drifted to class to start their day. This lifted my spirits daily and prompted me to smile and wave at both students and staff as I walked down the hallways. In this particular school, this was not a cultural norm, as reprimand seemed to best characterize daily interactions between students and good but overwhelmed staff. This was sad to me. At the time, I surmised it probably seemed odd at best to staff and students under the conditions as this 220-pound bald dude strolled down the hallways, grinning and waving to everybody.

During the school day, instead of attempting to help "get it right" through corrective feedback to teachers and reprimands to the students as they transitioned during the day, I began to verbally recognize the handful of classes transitioning through the hallways who were following some proximity of school expectations. It wasn't so much that I had a purpose; it just made me feel good as if somehow I was fighting the negative culture as if it were an infection. "Look at this line! Are these fourth graders?" I'd ask, pointing out some of their specific behaviors, knowing darn well they were only kindergartners. In response, the students proudly puffed out their chests and even put a "bubble" in their mouth as they paraded quietly to their next class. As the teacher walked by, I whispered something like, "I know this good transition didn't happen magically, very nice work!" I was sincere, and they appeared genuinely thankful for the recognition.

Members of my team soon began doing the same thing. What I started noticing was nothing short of amazing. When the students saw one of the team members in the hallways during transitions, more of them began progressively following expectations. As a result, the opportunity to deliver behavior-specific praise was increased. And praise in this culture was a commodity. In fact, when the teachers and staff saw me and one of my team members, we noticed more and more of them smiling, praising students, or gently reminding some of the transitioning expectations. Like a ripple effect, these positive behaviors began generalizing to other areas like the classroom, cafeteria, and playground, as if they were contagious. This was a stark contrast to the defeated body language and coercive type of interactions frequently observed during our initial observations. Misbehavior, I noticed, was still being corrected. And it absolutely should have been. But the quality of the interaction was visibly different as staff applied consequences using a business-like manner, effectively minimizing explosive student responses that typically resulted from corrections. And because the frequency of positive interactions had drastically increased, students seemed to be more accepting of the corrective feedback.

Soon the team and I began looking at the school's discipline data. To our delight, it reflected what they were seeing: drastic reductions in major discipline issues. In our excitement to spread the good news with the teachers, we shared a graph of the data with a brief note that said, "We've noticed many of you using behavior-specific praise with the students and correcting them in a calm manner when they misbehave. And guess what? Our discipline data reflects a 52 percent reduction in misbehavior. This is only 5 percent off this district's average. You guys rock! This is a huge accomplishment. We now are now in line with the school district's average." The teachers, delighted to see the data moving in the right direction, thanked us for sharing it and asked for the data to be pumped out weekly by grade groups so they could self-monitor. One teacher even noted, "Seeing that data move in the right direction is almost like getting paid! Not quite, but it makes me want to keep at it!" Pleased with the feedback and feeling similar to the teacher, the team and I began pumping out a five-question survey regarding the teacher's perspective on the support being provided to them. We were giving lots of feedback to the teachers, but they knew it was a two-way street. Feedback shouldn't be one way, but reciprocal so continuous improvement could occur. We knew that, for most people, perception is reality. This type of feedback, when sought out regularly, would allow us to act on suggestions, address any misperceptions discovered, and head off future issues, all the while ensuring folks were feeling supported.

To make a long story short, while the school made only modest achievement gains that year, improvement had clearly been made in the climate (i.e., shared staff perception) and culture (i.e., shared staff behavior), factors fundamental to future sustainability. In fact, the teachers, hearing the school was just 5 percent off the district average, decided they wanted to beat the average. And they did, smashing the number by another 20 percent, bringing them to a 70 percent reduction in discipline-related issues. And the cherry on top, the following year, the school made great academic achievement gains, an outcome that was undoubtedly tied to the momentum generated the previous year.

You might be thinking, "What's the purpose of this story? I don't work in schools. And besides, what the hell does it have to do with pinpointing anyhow?" The point is this: One little girl's smile had the power to change an entire school. Like a highly contagious healthy virus, it swept across the school and positively impacted a few critical behaviors of everybody that quickly led to other impactful behaviors. Those critical behaviors were simply smiling and providing behavior-specific praise. While smiling and praising often does produce positive behavioral karma, we aren't suggesting that smiling and praising people will solve all your problems. What's important to understand is that focusing on just a couple of the right behaviors in a given situation is often all that is needed to both generate momentum and reach desired goals.

Now, we've all experienced goals in one way or another. From setting personal goals at home to pursuing departmental and organizational goals at school or work, goal setting is a familiar and important concept. Bussinessdictionary.com (2019) defines a *goal* as "an observable and measurable end result having one or more objectives to be achieved within a more or less fixed time frame." We will discuss principles and hacks for goal setting that increase the likelihood they will be achieved in the next chapter. But for the purpose of this chapter on pinpointing, a goal can be described as the desired outcome of behavior, typically within a predetermined time frame (Fellner & Sulzer-Azaroff, 1984). This means, if we are to achieve goals, we must identify the very specific or *pinpointed* behaviors that will get us to a very specific or *pinpointed* result. And if we are to solve problems preventing us from achieving goals, we must first pinpoint exactly what the root cause of the issues is to effectively overcome them and pinpoint critical behaviors that will lead to the pinpointed results. While words like *locate, identify, determine,* and *isolate* are synonyms, we believe the term *pinpoint* to be apropos, as it suggests both discovery and precision as it relates to behavior and results.

Unfortunately, lots of people set goals, but never clearly define and then engage in the specific or pinpointed behavior or chain of behaviors required to achieve them. Whether it's a New Year's resolution or an organization finalizing what they want to achieve, much thought is placed on determining the goal, with too little thought placed on the systems, processes, and tasks required to achieve them. And while systems are made up of processes, and processes made up of tasks, it is *behavior* that makes up tasks; therefore, pinpointing *behavior* remains fundamental to the achievement of goals.

Critical Behavior

And we aren't simply talking about any behavior. Rather, high-impact behavior. These are the critical behaviors that will accelerate the attainment of goals and naturally recruit other behaviors in order to get the job done. In the science, there a certain classification of critical behaviors called *pivotal behaviors* that are important to understand. Pivotal behaviors are behaviors that when learned, lead to new and untrained behavior. This is important because choosing a pivotal behavior can accelerate learning, performance, and achievement of outcomes for you and others. Examples of pivotal behaviors for life and leadership include:

- Asking questions – e.g., "How did you do that?"
- Asking for feedback – e.g., "How did I do?"
- Making choices – e.g., Deciding to do this instead of that.

- Observational learning – e.g., Learning from expert videos, as discussed earlier.
- Self-management – e.g., "Am I doing what I need to?"
- Self-initiation – e.g., Doing what needs to be done.

These are all high impact behavior that have a ton of immediate and long-term benefits. What's important to understand is that there are a lot of things people can and need to do to achieve desired outcomes; however, the behavior that requires the least effort and produces the largest and most immediate desired result typically wins the day. Unfortunately, when the cost of behavior or the effort required exceeds the value of the accomplishments or results or outcomes it produces (Gilbert, 2007), problems occur. Have you ever worked really hard and long at something, like a relationship, and felt like nothing got accomplished? Or perhaps you were spending a long time trying to fix something that was broken and just couldn't figure it out. In either case, at some point, you may have decided enough was enough. In behavior analysis, we call this process *ratio strain* whereby too much behavior is required with too little payoff. Under many conditions, the behavior simply stops. In the case of relationships, people stop trying and may even move onto another one. And if you can't fix something that is broken, you might pay to have somebody else fix it, or perhaps just get rid of it.

In the workplace, a different outcome might occur. Thomas F. Gilbert, founder of the field of human performance technology, reminds us that behavior in the workplace is a means, and its consequences, the end. Combined, they make up the performance. If an employee doesn't find value in the outcomes related to their behavior, they will do just enough to get by, as the behavior is under contingencies of negative reinforcement. And if the organization is paying more for the behavior than the results it produces, well, they might get rid of the employee. In either case, "Houston, we have a problem." When it comes to performance, the goal is typically to get more for less—that is, more desired results for less behavior. When the value of accomplishments exceeds the cost of behavior in the workplace, Gilbert calls it "worthy performance" as it provides ample return on investment to the organization (2007). And when the performance is also worthy to the employee, discretionary effort or going above and beyond will occur, which will accelerate both performance and achievement of desired results if the right behaviors have been pinpointed (Daniels & Daniels, 2004).

This is applicable to leading your own life as well. If you engage in the most efficient behaviors that lead to the most immediate and meaningful results, you will remain on the path to success. Consequently, it's incredibly important to pinpoint what outcome you want and then pinpoint what behaviors will lead to that result. Similarly, when goals aren't being achieved, you must be able to pinpoint exactly what behaviors need to occur more, less, or differently to achieve them. In short, we are talking about pinpointing the root cause of the problem, a simple behavior hack we will discuss shortly. For example, a boxing coach and fighter might set a goal of reducing the number of times they are struck with a left hook over a ninety-day period. Now, there are many ways to avoid a left hook. But the pinpointed behavior might be head movement that involves rolling under the hook, which leads to the pinpointed result of successfully avoiding the hook. And the pinpointed result in the form of a goal might be reducing the number of times the fighter is hit on average during sparring by 25 percent.

Task Analysis	
Step 1	
Step 2	
Step 3	
Step 4	
Step 5	

Figure 3: Task analysis breakdown

By pinpointing a behavior, the coach can now further task-analyze (i.e., break down a complex skill into the component skills) movements to make it easier for him or her to measure and provide detailed feedback on specific components to help shape the fighter's performance. By learning to roll under the hook, the fighter is provided ample repetition during training and sparring in discriminating the appropriate opportunities to engage in rolling. During these opportunities, the fighter must also engage in associated behaviors like footwork, posture, and the accompanying offensive techniques that result from good head movement. In other words, this pinpoint naturally recruits other important behaviors that didn't need to be taught.

Now, if the combat sports analogy doesn't make sense, consider the task of making a peanut butter and jelly sandwich. What are the steps to completing it? Perhaps you are thinking something like this (fig. 4):

Now, this seems like a no-brainer, right? Result: Peanut butter and jelly sandwich. Behaviors that achieve result: Steps 1–5. But consider this. How might this look different if you were teaching this to a child? Do they know what supplies to get? Do they know where to get them? Do they know how to spread peanut butter and jelly? Do they know how to put the pieces of bread together? This may seem silly, but you might end up with the peanut butter facing out on one side and the jelly on the other! When pinpointing behaviors required to achieve any result, you must consider the complexity of the task and the ability required of those to perform it. The complexity of the task and skills of the person(s) expected to perform it need to be taken into consideration when designing a task analysis. The simple formula is this: more complex + less skilled = greater detail.

Task Analysis	
Step 1	Get Supplies
Step 2	Spread peanut butter on one slice of bread
Step 3	Spread jelly on the other side of bread
Step 4	Put the slices together
Step 5	Cut in half

Figure 4: Task analysis breakdown of making a peanut butter and jelly sandwich

There is another critical aspect related to the goal examples above. As mentioned, motivation or what behavior analysts might call *establishing operations* (Michael, 1993) is essential to success, as it gets people to behave toward the desired goal. And when they behave, their behavior has the opportunity to be reinforced, especially when they measurably observe themselves moving toward the goal. If a fighter is getting walloped with hooks during training or in actual fights, it's easy to imagine that avoiding a hook would be its own source of motivation. So the behavior of rolling under the hook likely comes into contingencies of naturally occurring reinforcement each time a hook is avoided. In other words, because the hook was avoided, the fighter will likely engage in the rolling behavior again in the future to achieve the same outcome. If the fighter engages in this behavior frequently and successfully avoids hooks, the fighter will likely develop a very important and healthy habit in the context of combat sports. In contrast, if somebody doesn't care for peanut butter and jelly sandwiches, they likely won't be motivated to engage in the behaviors required to make the sandwich. Under these conditions, naturally occurring reinforcement won't take over. This is where contriving reinforcement may be needed. For example, they might hate peanut butter, but they love money. So paying them $50 to eat the sandwich might achieve the desired result, but the behavior will undoubtedly go away as soon as the $50 incentive is removed! We will talk more about naturally occurring and contrived reinforcers during the chapter on pay for performance. But what's essential to understand in both cases is that there must be reinforcement available if behavior is going to occur.

SMART to SMARTER

Given the importance of motivation, it's odd that more focus isn't placed on it when developing goals. In fact, from a behavioral perspective, the primary purpose of setting goals should be to create additional opportunities for reinforcement (Daniels & Daniels, 2006). This has never been more evident than when we analyze the acronym SMART, a common approach to developing goals. A SMART goal, according to many authors (e.g., Doran, 1981), is one that is specific, measurable, achievable, results-focused, and timebound. Now, while these are all important aspects of goal setting, no component in there is suggestive of motivation. What if the goal isn't important to you or folks in an organization charged with achieving it, in the same way eating the peanut butter and jelly sandwich was motivating in the story above? If we are to achieve goals, or if we want others to achieve goals, we must ensure ample motivation is paired with the ability to engage in the behavior required to achieve them.

As such, the SMART acronym (specific, motivational, achievable, relevant, and trackable), as defined by Geller (2003), seems to make for a better fit given it addresses motivation. And rather than apply it only to goals, we'd suggest that focus be placed on developing SMART pinpoints as well (Gavoni & Weatherly, 2019). SMART pinpoints are:

- **Specific** – The result and behaviors required to achieve it are precise and observable.
- **Motivational** – The result needs to be meaningful if you or somebody else are to engage in the behavior required to achieve them.
- **Achievable** – Pinpoints need to be achievable. If it can't be done, or if doing it won't achieve the desired results, they aren't SMART at all!
- **Relevant** – There are many behaviors that can be selected from. But the behavior needs to be germane to day to day activities, and the results need to be connected to established goals.
- **Trackable** -Both pinpointed behaviors and results must be measurable. Period. If it can't be measured, it's not a pinpoint.

Thankfully, good pinpoints allow for solid measurement through leading and lagging indicators. And if you can measure it, you can move it! *Leading indicators* are metrics that let you know about the here and now and allow you to predict where you are going in terms of future performance, whereas *lagging indicators* are more like benchmarks that allow you to reflect on where you've gone in terms of past performance. The best leaders focus on leading indicators to remain agile in their decision-making. Bill Gates illustrated the concept well during his discussion about the economy and education when he said, "In the long run, your human capital is your main base of competition. Your leading indicator of where you're going to be twenty years from now is how well you're doing in your education system." Check out this pyramid of leading and lagging indicators as it pertains to safety in an organization as a simple visual to help you to better understand the concept.

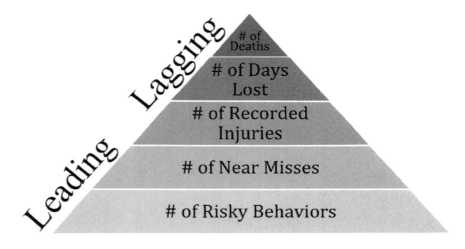

Figure 5

Pinpointing leading and lagging indicators as a measure of progress and source of reinforcement can be extremely powerful. Using leading indicators as predictive analytics has the potential to save you a lot of time and money, as it can let you know how things might turn out if things continue on the same trajectory. Similarly, using lagging indicators to reflect and make changes as necessary can help you stay the course or make changes as needed. We'll dig deeper into measurement when we discuss self-monitoring as one of the 5 scientific laws related to success.

As we mentioned at the beginning of this chapter, failure to establish SMART pinpoints related to both the outcome and the behavior required to achieve it is often at the root of the failure to achieve success. Remember, all results require somebody doing something more, less, or differently. Setting a goal in and of itself is insufficient for achieving it. If you want to achieve personal goals or support the attainment of goals in your organization, you need to pinpoint behavior and results so that you have a way to measure and reinforce progress. Sometimes the reinforcement is simply observing yourself moving in the right direction (i.e., a leading indicator). So, don't settle for just establishing goals. Make sure you take the time to develop SMART pinpoints to help you achieve your goals.

Pinpointing the Root Cause of Performance Issues—Can't Do vs. Won't Do

It's Monday morning and the executive team is reviewing performance data over the last week. "I'm looking at David's productivity. He's not getting the job done. Neither are Anne and Carlos. What's going on?" asks the senior leader in earnest. "Oh, those three," responds a manager. "They're hopeless and incompetent. We should just get rid of them."

Does this scenario sound familiar? If you've worked in any profession long enough, you've likely heard different versions of the same complaint. This story is not uncommon. You know, grumblings like, "They aren't doing their job," "They aren't holding up their end," or, "I told them what to do and they still aren't doing it." Blame, blame, BLAME! We've all heard this, and most of us have likely said it ourselves. Some even hurl adjectives like "lazy," "useless," "weak," or perhaps "ridiculous," as frustration sets in when staff aren't performing as expected. Soon fingers are pointed and feelings hurt, and all the while nothing changes. And in some cases, large sums of money are dumped into training as the assumption is made that staff have not been trained properly. This cycle repeats itself in many organizations across the country.

In the example above, let's say the leader "knows" the employee was trained, as they recently went to a professional development related to the task. We say "know" because the wisest of you are very aware that just because somebody has participated in training doesn't mean they have been trained or are able to perform successfully on the job! There is the misconception that once an employee receives training, they will be able to demonstrate competency and fluency with those identified repertoires the leader is trying to increase.

Here's the thing, some investigators have found that training components of theory and discussion lead to only a 10 percent increase in knowledge and a 5 percent increase in the performance of targeted skills within the training session (Joyce & Showers, 2002). Simply put, telling somebody what to do and even talking it through with them results in little return on investment. Remember, the goal is typically for knowledge and skills learned in the training environment to translate into improved performance in the actual work environment. So, what percentage of those skills instructed and modeled within the training session do you think translate into actual application within the work environment? Unfortunately, in this study, that number was found to be 0 percent.

Training devoid of the key components of instruction, modeling, and lots of practice with feedback frequently leads to dismal outcomes. Repertoires taught using the methodology of only theory and discussion do not typically translate into practice within the organizational setting. Regrettably, this is the core training methodology of *many* professional development programs. Clearly, when it comes to pinpointing performance issues, it's important that folks know what they are supposed to be doing and how to do it. However, one of the biggest assumptions (often a costly one) about performance issues is that training is *the answer* to improving outcomes. Before deciding if training is going to be part of the intervention, leaders should determine if there are other factors that may be a barrier to a person performing well. Unfortunately, in most organizations, this determination typically comes in the form of performance evaluations that do little to help people pinpoint the root cause of a performance issue.

Though considered a necessary evil by many, performance evaluations in countless organizations seem to have become the go-to move for assessing and providing feedback to improve performance. Even with the best intentions, these evaluations frequently end up doing more harm than good, as they are often dreaded by employees and leaders alike. If it were up to us, and we actually regularly do this in our weekly interactions in the form of reciprocal feedback, we'd replace evaluations with simple coaching strategies rooted in the behavioral science that focus on improving performance in the moment, not evaluating it long after it has occurred. At any rate, evaluations might be useful in telling you what the employees aren't doing, but they are typically useless for telling you why.

Case in point, a leader observes two new employees within the same organization. Unfortunately, neither employee is performing a certain task to an acceptable standard. In fact, on the 0–5 evaluation scale, they'd both receive a 1 to indicate the employees' performance is at a beginning level. So now what? Does the leader send the employees to training? Do they model for them? Do they spend valuable time coaching them? How should this situation be approached?

To say that poorly performing staff will negatively impact the attainment of important goals is an understatement in organizations that fail (Daniels & Bailey, 2014). Similarly, if you don't do the right things, in the right ways, at the right time, you will fail to reach your personal goals. Good leaders go beyond recognizing that poor performance is occurring. They seek to understand why it is occurring so they can effectively support change—that is, support behavior change of an employee, or behavior change of themselves. When you or somebody else aren't performing to a standard, there is always a reason beyond "lazy" or any of the choice adjectives noted above. **Simply put, it comes down to a "can't do" it or a "won't do" it.** More accurately put, there is either a skill deficit or a performance deficit.

But how does one determine this without painstaking and time-consuming assessments? Don't despair! Organizational Behavior Management (OBM) practitioners have already developed a simple tool that can help. This tool, known as the Performance Diagnostic Checklist (Carr et al., 2013), contains a series of simple questions that can be used to pinpoint the root cause of performance issues.

PDC - The Ultimate Behavior Hack for Diagnosing and Pinpointing Performance Issues

The PDC is typically used by OBM practitioners to collect data for performance analysis. Remember the three-term contingency called the ABC formula from earlier (i.e., antecedents, behavior, consequences)? The PDC unpacks this formula as it relates to performance issues to allow us to understand functionally why performance is occurring to a standard, except it adds a fourth contingency, *motivating operations.*

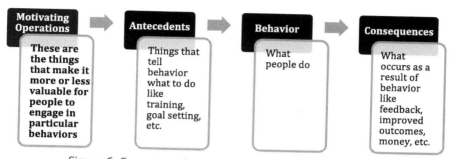

Figure 6: Four-term Contingency: Motivating Operations

The initial motivation to engage in behavior is very important. If people don't behave, there is no way they can produce valued outcomes. A simple way to look at motivating operations is to think about when people are deprived of things they want or need. In this case, their motivation will increase for those things. In contrast, when people have too much of something or have a certain level of satiation, their motivation will decrease for those same things. It's important to understand this because it affects how people respond when certain antecedents are present or presented. For example, even with the greatest training, if somebody doesn't value the outcomes of performing, they aren't very likely to engage in the behavior. A simpler example is hunger. If you are really hungry, you are likely willing to drive or even walk to the nearest restaurant to eat. Depending on how hungry you are (i.e., state of deprivation), you might be willing to drive or walk very far! However, if you are full (i.e., sated), you probably aren't very motivated to walk or drive to the restaurant to get food, even if the restaurant is right next door!

Fortunately, using the PDC is the ultimate behavior hack for navigating the four-term contingency and getting to the bottom of why somebody isn't performing a certain task well. It's not a complicated process and can be used by anybody, including leaders, as it is simply a brief questionnaire that does not require a lot of time and effort. The pay-off can be huge, as the individual data can be utilized to pinpoint the root causes of performance issues of an employee, and the aggregate data can be used to identify the root cause of performance issues of groups of employees so that an appropriate and effective intervention can be applied. In the appendix, we have included a slightly modified version of the PDC (Carr & Wilder, 2015) that can be used to determine both performance deficits and the appropriate interventions within your organization. There is no doubt that you will want to keep this in your toolbox for diagnosing the performance problems of others—and yourself! Let's briefly review some of the important antecedents and consequences as they relate to pinpointing performance issues using the PDC.

Pinpointing Antecedent Issues

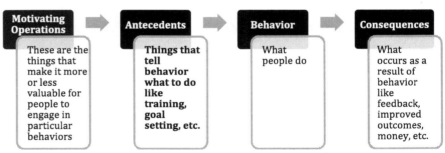

Figure 7: Four-term Contingency: Antecedents

As we've reviewed, when employees fail to perform, many people tend to point their finger at them; however, as you can see, the PDC pinpoints a variety of practical root causes related to areas like antecedents and training, knowledge and skills, processes, and motivation. A big part of the motivation piece is linked to approaches related to observation and feedback by the leader.

The PDC can be used to target antecedent strategies (i.e., strategies used to get behavior going) like training, task clarification, prompting, adjusting materials, processes, etc. There are times when simply giving an employee equipment, stating the specific skill a leader wants the employees to engage in or reminding them to engage in it prior to an observation increases the likelihood they will perform. However, if giving people supplies and telling them what to do was all it took to be successful in leadership and life, you wouldn't be reading this book! The goal of any antecedent strategies is to get an employee or yourself to successfully engage in a specific skill and experience positive outcomes as a result. For example, if a manager uses a specific management strategy like task clarification and observes her employees performing better as in the example above, there is a good chance she will use this strategy again in the future. Similarly, if after reading this book, you begin to use some of the suggested behavior hacks and you notice a positive difference, you are much more likely to continue using them.

Sometimes task clarification and prompting is all that is needed to get behavior going long enough so the employees can get in touch with some sort of naturally occurring reinforcement (i.e., something of value occurs as a result of the behavior). However, as a leader, you must remember this: training, task clarification, prompting, and all of the other strategies that come before a behavior are antecedents. In other words, they come before the behavior occurs. While antecedent strategies are extremely important and part of the ABC formula for performance improvement, remember that these strategies only serve to get behavior moving in the right direction; it's what occurs after the behavior that ensures it will be maintained.

Consequently, as we've detailed in earlier chapters, it is partly the job of the leader to create opportunities for employees to practice critical behaviors correctly, receive feedback, and experience positive reinforcement in the natural environment to ensure the development of habits that lead to positive outcomes. Similarly, as a leader of your own life, you must create similar opportunities to engage in and improve your own behaviors if you are to achieve success. There are a variety of ways people do this formally and informally through education, self-help books, training, videos, podcasts, etc.

Pinpointing Consequence Issues

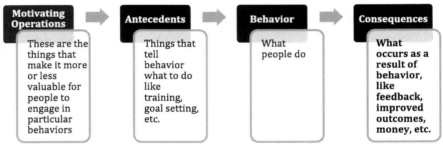

Figure 8: Four-term Contingency: Consequences

The PDC is a road map that will help you determine the next steps for performance improvement that will ultimately lead to goal achievement. When using the PDC, you may find that training is, in fact, not the appropriate intervention for the issue. It may be implementing a simple visual support to remind the employee of what it is they need to do, as sometimes the issue is that the employee merely hasn't gotten into the *habit* of performing a certain skill. We all fall prey to this when learning something new, as habits take time to change. However, this is actually good news, as the modus operandi for intervention is typically related to that time-consuming and cost-prohibitive option of training, as we highlighted earlier. And while this might be a good strategy when an employee has a skill deficit (i.e., can't do it), professional development is a complete waste of time when employees actually possess the required skills.

Sometimes it's not a "can't do" issue, but more of a "won't do" directly related to consequences. Without coaching and feedback delivered frequently and immediately, or without the ability for the employee to observe positive outcomes related to a certain task, desirable and long-lasting behavior linked to goal attainment will not occur. If an employee possesses the skill but is not using it, one area that must be measured in the way feedback is being delivered. When we say feedback, we mean all feedback—not just corrective or constructive, but also reinforcing feedback that helps an employee align their behavior with positive outcomes. Reinforcement is key here. The employee may have the skills but lack the motivation to engage in the behavior because they are not able to observe meaningful outcomes that result from it.

When improving motivation through reinforcing consequences, an intervention may be as simple as providing direct feedback or leaving a note on their desk or sending a brief memo that says, "I really like the way you've increased the delivery of behavior-specific praise to your supervisees. As a result, I've noticed both improved performance and morale, as indicated by the recent surveys. This is at the root of great management. Keep up the great work!" The point is that the leader is helping the employee, a manager, in this case, align their behavior with meaningful outcomes.

And here's the best part: as a leader in an organization (or a parent, best friend, spouse, significant other, son or daughter), you can use the PDC as a self-assessment to make sure those you support are receiving the required support. For example, "Have I ensured the employee has been provided training?" "Have I ensured the employee has the needed materials?" Or perhaps, "Am I ensuring the employee is being observed and receiving regular, positive feedback?" And as a leader of your own life, you can easily use the PDC as a diagnostic to figure out why you might not be reaching your own personal goals that move you closer to who and what you value. For example: "Have I been properly trained?" "Have I taught my child how to do it?" "Can I clearly state what I should do to reach this goal?" "Do I have the materials and processes to achieve my goal?" "Does my husband have all the equipment he needs to finish the job?" "Have I prioritized the right tasks to reach my goal?" "Did I let my child know what they are doing well and then provide helpful feedback where needed?" Or perhaps, "Am I using self-monitoring as a feedback mechanism that lets me know if I'm moving toward my goal?"

Clearly knowing what to do is essential to success. But knowing isn't just about having knowledge. Central to the definition of knowing is awareness. In other words, are you aware of what you are doing, how you are doing it, why you are doing it, when you are doing it, who are you doing it with, and the impact of what you are doing? Being aware of your behavior and the impact of it is fundamental to producing positive behavioral karma. We will dive deep into that in our chapter on self-monitoring. In the meantime, let's take a quick look at actual pinpointing through a shared story that we will continue by connecting it with goal setting in the next chapter.

Pinpointing After Diagnostics – Brett & Paulie's Story

A very specific example of how we used both antecedent information and consequence information to help us pinpoint and resolve a problem occurred in early 2019. After analyzing the most recent data, we recognized a very small division of our company was not performing to our quality standards for supporting learners on the autism spectrum; moreover, they were underperforming in terms of the revenue generated required for sustainability. Our data allowed us to pinpoint the following issues: (1) appropriate hours to fulfill contracts were less than satisfactory, and (2) employees were only working at 20 percent capacity. As a result, the learners were not receiving the number of hours they were entitled to, and colleagues were fighting amongst themselves, which magnified poor services to such a vulnerable population of students. To rectify this, we used one simple hack: leaders of this division were required to precisely measure the work hours completed and simply graphically display and share the data via text to all employees of the company.

This real-life story illustrates well how we were able to pinpoint the issue along with specific behaviors to improve the quality of services being provided to vulnerable learners. The behaviors and results were specific, motivational, attainable, relevant, and trackable. In short, SMART!

KEY TAKEAWAYS:

- » All results require behavior to achieve them.
- » When pinpointing results and behavior, think SMART.
- » Identify and focus on only the most critical behaviors required to achieve a result.
- » When possible, identify pivotal behaviors.
- » Break complex tasks into smaller, easier to manage components or chunks.
- » Identify leading and lagging indicators to measure progress and accomplishments.
- » When poor performance is occurring, it is either a can't do or a won't do.

ASK YOURSELF:

- » What do I or others want to accomplish?
- » What do I or others need to do to accomplish it?
- » Is the accomplishment worthy of the effort? In other words, is it motivational?
- » Do I or others know what to do, how to do it, and when to do it?
- » Am I monitoring or self-monitoring performance?
- » If I or others engage in the pinpointed behavior, how will I/we be able to measure progress?

CHAPTER 6

Goal Setting Using Science

While pinpointing is essential to success, oftentimes, goals serve as what we call a *discriminative stimulus* to achieve those goals. A discriminative stimulus or SD is what behavioral scientists call "a stimulus in the presence of which a particular response will be reinforced" (Malott, 2007). You might think of it simply as something that, when present, reminds you what behavior you should engage in. Like when you see a red light, you stop. Your behavior of stopping is likely reinforced because you avoid tickets and accidents.

The most effective leaders focus on achieving goals by helping people develop the ability to do the right thing in the right way across varied situations so that the behavior is met with positive reinforcement. Helping a child learn math so they can solve math equations, helping a teenager learn to drive, or helping an employee learn to perform their job effectively all typically lead to outcomes that are valued. As you now know, when these behaviors occur consistently and are linked to valued outcomes, they eventually become a habit. As we've suggested, the goal of leaders should be to design and apply strategies that accelerate the development and sustainability of good habits. And as a leader of your own life or perhaps in your household or relationship, this applies to you reaching your own goals or supporting those you care for with reaching theirs.

Goal Setting – Brett & Paulie's Story

Once we pinpointed the issue & desired results related to our small division not performing to our quality standards for supporting vulnerable learners, we then pinpointed the exact behaviors we wanted the division leaders to engage in and gathered baseline data. With data in hand, we set an appropriate and attainable daily collective goal for all employees to strive for that was simply 10 percent above the currently utilized hours. To illustrate this goal, the leader would then draw a simple yellow line on the graphic display. As we noted before, these graphs and the goal were distributed via text message to all employees of the division. An amazing synergy among the team led by Jason Golowski began manifesting from the process. We saw positive comments all throughout the text message threads by colleagues complimenting each other and reinforcing teamwork toward this goal. We will return to this story in the next chapter.

In Home & Preschool Hours Combined

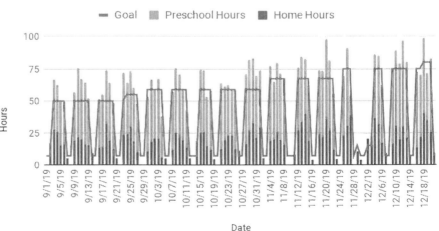

Figure 9: Changing Criterion Design - Goal Achievement

But before we can think about helping ourselves or others reach goals, we must consider the most powerful source of motivation— the *why* or what we truly value. Behaviorally speaking, values involve verbally constructed contingencies (i.e., if I do this, then this will occur) that function to both inform us of our behavior related to them and motivate us to behave toward them (Hayes et al., 1999). In relation to the four-term contingency discussed in chapter 3, they serve as an establishing operation, as they increase the likelihood that you or others will engage in a particular behavior or behaviors. Think about parents. Because they value their children's health, they will engage in a number of behaviors to ensure their child is getting the nutrients they need, often beginning in utero! And when leaders create a strong vision for their followers, they will be motivated to do almost anything—even fight in wars.

In his book *Start with Why: How Great Leaders Inspire Everyone to Take Action,* Simon Sinek reminds us that whether we are leaders in an organization or in our own lives, we must start with a purpose or vision—essentially, the "why." Much like we discussed, determining a valued result and then the behaviors required to achieve it, Sinek reminds us not to worry so much about the route until you make sure you have a destination in mind. As long as you know where you want to go, you will find a way to get there. Unfortunately, many of us fall into our careers and end up living our lives by accident. We see it all the time as college students think of their degree as the end result, rather than a benchmark moving them toward a true purpose. Or in many cases, people chase the money. Listen, we all have to pay the bills, and we'd all like certain luxuries life has to offer. We get it. And to a certain point, money does equate to happiness. But there is a cap. In a study published in the *Nature of Human Behaviour,* a sample of over 1.7 million individuals worldwide showed emotional well-being is directly related to income until around $60,000–$75,000 (Jeb, Tay, Diener & Oishi, 2018).

We think it's a shame that many people continue to pursue happiness by continuing to chase the money, even when some have plenty of it! If lots of money made people happy, many of the reality shows that exploit the rich, famous, and *sad* wouldn't exist. Lots of people make decisions on what they will do based on the amount of money it will make them. Early in life, we did. At the end of the day, though, we believe it is the pursuit of both meaning and happiness that is most meaningful and brings out the best in people. Finding meaning and happiness requires you to understand both what you are good at and what you truly value. Many people don't. In the absence of values, people tend to behave in ways that are socially acceptable, bring them positive attention, get them in touch with primary reinforcers like food, water, sleep, and sex, and allow them to avoid things that make them feel bad (Bond, 2004). Think about it. We've all diverted from our goals to access things that had more immediate value. For example, you behave a certain way because it's the "way things are done around here," or you dress a certain way because it brings desired attention. Most people don't want to look weird, and many of us do desire positive attention. We'd be lying if we said we didn't. Or perhaps you succumb to the all-powerful primal needs of food, drink, and sex. *Excessively*. We've personally fallen to all of these—in spades. It's not unusual for many people to be derailed by these same yearnings. But those who have a powerful vision, purpose, mission, or why are rarely derailed. And when they are, they find themselves pulled back on the tracks through the strength of their why. Knowing your why helps you to forgo small immediate reward to gain access to larger, more remote fulfilling reinforcers.

Finding Your Niche

When you find your true niche, you have essentially discovered a job or activity that you are good at, enjoy engaging in, and links directly to your why. As Aubrey Daniels, the godfather of organizational behavior management, is fond of saying, "Behavior goes where reinforcement flows." In everyday terms, this just means we will engage in behaviors that result in valued outcomes—in other words, behaviors that produce reinforcement. If you are good at your job or activity, you like doing it, and it moves you toward your why. That's a lot of reinforcement that will sustain your behavior and likely recruit others that will continue to make you better. Given the potential power of a niche, let's take a look at two behavior hacks we hope might get you started in finding your niche.

Behavior Hack #1 - Discover Your Aptitude

> SUCCESS IS NOT FINAL, FAILURE IS NOT FATAL:
> IT IS THE COURAGE TO CONTINUE THAT COUNTS.

You must discover your aptitude. If we were physicists, we might describe aptitude as "potential energy that is stored within you." Some people just get some things. It happened with us in behavior analysis. We love the science. It just makes sense. But that doesn't mean we get everything. For example, we aren't researchers, and writing academically is like pulling teeth, as it just doesn't seem to come naturally to us. There are many aspects to any field that require a specialized skill set that you might have. Maybe training comes naturally to you, or perhaps developing procedures. Maybe it's coaching or leading others. Or perhaps you are really good at communicating and might be a great public speaker. Here's the thing, if you are going to discover your aptitude, you must try things out. Some people never tap into their potential energy or aptitude because they limit their experiences. These types of people and there are many of them, allow their fear of failure to paralyze them from trying new things. As a result, they never find their niche, as their focus remains on maintaining a "safe" life and never really discovering their aptitude.

As decent combat athletes, we ended up winning titles and having the opportunity to compete on national television. Now, we were both very kind and compassionate kids. Not aggressive at all as we avoided fights and were even bullied. Nobody would have ever pegged us as fighters. Nobody would have known we had an aptitude in this area had we not overcome our own inner demons and eventually gone to the gym to give it a try.

Similarly, there was a time when we were both deathly afraid of public speaking. Had we not tried it and stuck with it through the large amount of anxiety we experienced, we would have never discovered that we have an apparent aptitude for that as well! So while you must do an assessment of what you do well, there are other things to consider. What do people typically search you out for? Are you a good listener? Do people seem to value your advice? Do you give exceptional training? Are there other skills you've considered developing? While you may not have thought about that, take a look around. What is it that other people do that you wish you could? And of those skills, which do you think you would be best at? And which do you think you would struggle with? We just want to note this: if they can do it, you can do it too! As behavior analysts, we know that with the right training and coaching rooted in the science, anybody can improve their performance. This means you! But being good at something is only part of the formula. If you are to regularly engage in a behavior and be the best you can be, you know there must be ample motivation. So let's take a look at that.

Behavior Hack #2 – Find Your Why

When determining what you want to do, you need to be real with yourself. Are you doing it for the money, or are you doing it because of the sense of satisfaction you get as a result of your performance? Remember, Simon Sinek reminds us to start with the *why*. In this case, what is your why or your passion? As you know from the last chapter's discussion on the four-term contingency, a why might be thought of as an *establishing operation* or an environmental variable that increases the value of a stimulus, object, or event as a reinforcer and increases the frequency in behavior that provides access to the reinforcer (Cooper, Heron & Heward, 2007). More simply put, it creates a want that results in you behaving in ways to access what you desire. Recall, behavior goes where reinforcement flows. When you know your why and can see yourself moving toward it, your behavior becomes sustainable. This is because the results your behavior produces become reinforcing as you observe yourself measurably getting closer and closer to a valued outcome. When it comes to finding out what's important to an organization, you can often tell by observing where their resources are allocated. Similarly, you can take a look at your own life to see where you invest your time and your money. What types of things do you engage in, or do you see others engage in, that just make you feel good? You know these things. When you are engaged in or observing these activities, time just seems to fly by.

It's not unusual for somebody to be asked what their vision is. The problem is, many people don't know! For many of these good folks, you would find that money has been the primary driving reinforcer in their lives, not passion. If you are trying to find passion and think only about money or only within your current circumstances, you are boxing yourself in. Think about anything, anywhere that regularly captures your attention. And don't just limit yourself to things you desire to participate in. Pay attention to topics you find yourself regularly attending to. Ask yourself what it is about that topic that interests you, then envision what it would be like to be engaged in the related activities and experiencing the outcomes they produce.

Meaning Not Money

Listen, as leaders and coaches, we've been able to successfully apply the science in business, education, and sports and across relationships. While we failed often, our passion and vision kept us moving forward, finding a way around or through obstacles. As we reflect, we both recognized that it made us happy to help people and that people regularly sought us out to help them because we were, well, helpful we'd surmise. You can do the same. Be a behavior detective and reflect on your experiences, your behavior, and your values. What are you good at, or what might you be good at? And what do you find meaning in? An essential hack for long-term sustained performance is to focus on making meaning, not money. Once you understand this, you are on your way. Now, while you can't just drop your existing job, you can begin cracking the door open in the area you desire to make an impact in. This will require additional effort on your part. But the beautiful thing is, when you are pursuing your passion, it doesn't feel effortful. It's exciting. The pursuit of money at best will mitigate frustrations in your career. But if you "do what you love," as the old saying goes, "you will never work a day in your life." Besides, if you find a job you love, you will be good at it, and oftentimes matching aptitude with passion and purpose in a career can be associated with financial reward.

When you lead your life or an organization with purpose, it means you understand the direction you're heading, but you remain open to the route. You understand your values, you set goals, and you determine your pinpoints, that is, pinpointing exactly where you want to go based on your purpose or vision, and then pinpointing the exact behaviors that will get you there. Given that a purpose or vision is typically a long-term venture, it's important to have goals all along the way to help keep behavior moving in the right direction. And when people share a vision, it fosters collaboration, safety, trust, and motivation to engage in behaviors required to meet communal goals. The result: massive doses of positive behavioral karma!

In chapter 3, we discussed the development of SMART pinpoints to achieve personal and organizational goals. Identifying the precise results and critical behaviors required to achieve a goal is key to making it happen. Like any worker trying to make it to the job on time, they must first know where they are, determine their destination, and know the specific route they will travel. They must also possess the prerequisite skills to drive and then have sufficient motivation to actually drive to the predetermined location.

Unfortunately, ample motivation alone doesn't quite cut it. Saying, "I really need to lose fifteen pounds," doesn't ensure you will meet that goal. Even if you really mean it! While it might be enough to get you moving in the right direction, it isn't enough to sustain the behavior required to meet goals, especially when these are long-term goals. As you know, this requires sufficient reinforcement of the behaviors required to achieve the goals. Without a reinforcing consequence, there is no behavior. The problem is that life gets in the way and too often, the wrong behaviors end up contacting reinforcement. Behaviorally speaking, we mean that competing reinforcers get in the way of achieving goals (Winston, & Redd, 1976). You've been there. We all have in one form or another.

Take the weight loss example above. Most of us want to lose a few pounds or more. Perhaps you are focusing on your health or maybe you desire to look like that guy or gal on the cover of your favorite magazines. One morning, after devouring the local buffet the night before, you try to squeeze into your clothes. Low and behold, your pants won't button, and your previously fitted shirt now looks like a shmedium (that means it's too tight!) on you. You hop on the scale, look down, and then proclaim to yourself or perhaps your significant other, "That's it, I'm going on a diet!" And you are dead serious. You are going to drop that damn weight! So you set a goal to lose five pounds by the end of the month and then head off about your business, determined to eat healthier and meet your goal.

And then, it happens: life. It's Friday night, you've eaten pretty clean during the week, and your besty asks you to go to happy hour. You haven't seen her in a while, so you happily oblige, indulging in the happy hour cocktails and few of the healthier finger foods available. You are having such a blast, you both decide to take the show on the road and head to the local nightclub to continue the party. WHAT A NIGHT!

The next morning, you roll out of bed, and it hits you: as really, really great as the night before was, your morning seems to be proportionally the opposite. It really, really sucks. If you could go back in time for approximately ten hours, you would tell the younger and less wise you to head home after a happy hour. Unfortunately, some wisdom must be learned the hard way. At any rate, you feel like crap as your head pounds like the music from last night, and your stomach seems to be warring with itself. You'd do anything to feel better. So you throw down a couple of Tylenol, and then your mind quickly shifts to what you are going to eat. In fact, you realize your body is craving food, as you remember you'd foregone a real dinner the night before for a liquid one. But it's not just craving any food. It's craving naughty food. The naughtiest. The kind of food you've stayed away from all week, and worse. So what do you do?

Well, most of us know how this story likely ends. We delay the attainment of a goal that is removed in time to get rid of the immediate crappy feeling. That means, eat junk food now and possibly return to the diet later. The science of human behavior could have predicted this, as people tend to behave in ways that garner the most certain and immediate reinforcement. In this case, getting rid of the headache and crappy feeling as soon as possible are negatively reinforcing, as you are removing aversives (i.e., headache and crappy feeling). It's not that you don't want to lose weight. It's just the delay in this positive consequence that can't compete with the bad feeling of now. In other words, the reinforcers available in life are here and now get in the way of there and later. Those who are successful are consistent in their behavior. Like the turtle who beats the hare, they maintain a steady pace to achieve success. They keep their eye on the prize.

So what can be done about this? How can we determine SMART pinpoints and then continue behaving in ways that help us reach our goals? Well, thankfully, a growing body of research behind acceptance commitment therapy (ACT) (Hayes et al., 2006) can help us improve self-control (behaviorally speaking, choosing a larger delayed consequence over a smaller, more immediate one) in order to move us toward what we value. ACT is a mindfulness approach that helps move us toward who and what we value as we learn to become better observers of our behavior and the impact of it. And ACT isn't just about what we do, but what we think as well. It can accelerate the attainment of goals by helping us reduce self-defeating thoughts (covert behavior) that tend to increase the likelihood we will engage in unproductive behavior or those behaviors that tend to move us away from our values. More on this in the next chapter on self-monitoring. To this point in the chapter, we've discussed finding your why as a critical element that underlies goal setting. Now let's look into a few behavior hacks for creating goals that will increase your positive behavioral karma.

Establishing SMART Goals

"So long as a person is committed to the goal, has the requisite ability to attain it, and does not have conflicting goals, there is a positive, linear relationship between goal difficulty and task performance" (Locke & Latham, 2006). And when these goals are specific and challenging, the performance of individuals has been found to increase up to 29 percent as compared with the performance of individuals who were provided general and easy goals (Locke & Latham, 1990). When people are motivated by and commit to relevant goals, they rise to the challenge (Erez & Zidon, 1984; Klein, Wesson, Hollenbeck, & Alge, 1999), as long as the goal is attainable and doesn't surpass the limits of their ability (Catania, 2007). Hmmm . . . *specific* goals that are *motivational, attainable,* and *relevant.* Given that they've been measured by the investigators, we can also assume they are *trackable.* Do you see a pattern here? Like the SMART pinpoints we explored earlier, the goals being discussed are also SMART!

Scientifically speaking, goals are stimuli that precede behavior and have discriminative control over the response, which increases the likelihood the behavior will occur again in the future (Fellner & Sulzer-Azaroff, 1984). When people link goal achievement and delayed consequences, like, "If I achieve this goal, then I will earn this reward later," a function-altering effect occurs on the consequences of performance-related behaviors. That is, setting goals can transfer moment-to-moment performance into reinforcing consequences of the behavior upon which performance depends (Fellows & Mawhinney, 1997). Simply put, I know doing this now will allow me to achieve or earn that later. So, doing this now is meaningful to me. And when goal attainment is actually paired with positive consequences or the removal of negative ones, goals can function as conditioned positive or negative reinforcing stimuli.

As such, SMART goals can be extremely powerful for engaging people, including yourself, in movement toward and the eventual attainment of desired outcomes. According to Macey et al. (2009), "the feeling of engagement cannot occur without a specific purpose or objective." For example, in everyday life, some people choose to pursue formal education. Those who are successful are driven by a larger vision. For example, perhaps they would like to become a teacher, lawyer, engineer, or behavior analyst. This larger purpose or objective is powerful enough to get college students to sacrifice more immediate reinforcers like watching television, hanging out with friends, or earning wages in a full-time job, and engage in the day-to-day grind associated with college. As they move toward their degree, they hit a variety of SMART goals and subgoals, like completing a paper, getting a good grade on a test, and earning a good grade in the class.

When it comes to leadership, if engagement is to occur, Macey et al. (2009) recognize the need for alignment between individual goals and organizational goals, hence the *M* for *motivational* in the SMART acronym. This makes good sense as if there is a disconnect between organizational and employee values, employees are far less likely to independently engage in tasks required to achieve goals. For example, part of our vision is disseminating the science of human behavior across the world, a vision shared by our behavioral ambassadors who make up our branding team. One of the goals we regularly set with our branding team is increasing the number of people we are able to influence across social media. At last check, we are around a quarter of a million folks, which started from zero. By setting regular goals (e.g., moving the metric from 200,000 to 210,000) and providing the tools and resources to move that metric (e.g., content experts, film crew, editors, etc.), we regularly hit goals and then celebrate successful attainment in a variety of ways.

To increase the likelihood you will achieve a goal, you must identify your SMART pinpoints and a couple of simple measures aligned with the SMART goal. For example, if the desired result was losing weight:

- SMART goal: Lose 15 pounds
  - Sub-goals: 1.5 pounds weekly

- SMART pinpoints: Eat fewer carbs, eat more protein, exercise more. To be most effective, these pinpoints would need to be more precise. For example, determining exactly how many carbs, grams of protein, and types and hours of exercise.
  - Measure: Scale, how clothing fits, the measure of waist, arms, legs, etc., and self-monitoring carb/protein intake and spending hours at the gym.

While this is simple, the approach is actually rooted in scientific principles that will increase the likelihood of goal achievement. In this case, losing fifteen pounds. And there are a variety of reinforcers (the *M* in SMART) that sustain the behavior required to lose weight. For example, clothing fits better, compliments from people, a general sense of improved well-being, etc. In another example related to increasing employee retention, an organization might set a SMART goal of increasing the number of employees satisfied by 20 percent.

- SMART goal: Improve the number of satisfied employees by 20 percent.
  - Sub-goals: 5 percent increase monthly.
- SMART pinpoint: Increase the frequency of positive feedback delivered by managers and supervisors.
  - Measure: Surveys, direct observations, self-monitoring, retention.

Common errors made when setting goals are making them too large (violating the attainable rule), failing to identify accurate pinpoints (violating the specificity rule), and failing to identify regular metrics that can be regularly observed as a measure of progress (violating the trackable rule). This is why it's critical that your goals are SMART! Let's look at a couple of behavior hacks that will help you along the way.

Build It and They Will Come

As you can see, the SMARTer your goals, the more likely you or others will be to engage in the behaviors required to achieve them, and the more positive behavioral karma you will produce. And the SMARTer your pinpoints and the more deliberate your leadership or self-monitoring is, the more you help yourself or the people you support to develop good habits. Like Kevin Costner's famous quote *from Field of Dreams*, "If you build it, they will come," building behavior will bring results. Remember, no result is achieved without behavior, so it's critical that behavior is the central focus of your efforts, not results. If you get the behavior right, the results will come. Here are a couple of critical behaviors to move you in the right direction for developing habits:

Behavior Hacks for Achieving Goals

Behavior Hack #1 – Set Subgoals

In their eagerness to achieve large success, many leaders tend to set large goals. Unfortunately, much like the Hail Mary in football, these goals tend to fall short of their mark. This can have a negative impact on morale and performance, as folks are failing to get in touch with reinforcement through the successful attainment (remember the *A* in SMART!) of goals. The simple behavior hacks: set smaller goals. For instance, in the weight loss example above, instead of determining one longer-term goal of losing 15 pounds, you will note the 15 pounds is broken down into a number of subgoals of 1.5 pounds weekly. An example of setting subgoals is exactly what happened with this book.

I (Brett) don't particularly like to read and write in long durations. However, Paulie suggested I read one page and let him know what I thought. As I write this, I realized it created behavioral momentum, and now I have read and responded to at least fifty pages. Furthermore, right now on 10/19/19 at 9:25 p.m. in the evening, Paulie set a small short-term (sub) goal for me to read and discuss two pages with him. Subsequently, he had to end the call and spend time with his family, but it resulted in behavioral momentum, and I continued reading and writing through another twenty pages. If Paulie had not set the small short-term goal of two pages, I'm certain I would not have written these exact words to expedite the publication of this book. These subgoals can then be celebrated as they are achieved, and motivation sustained through the regular reinforcement associated with moving toward the ultimate goal.

Behavior Hack #2 – Quick Wins

> THE ELEVATOR TO SUCCESS IS OUT OF ORDER.
> YOU'LL HAVE TO USE THE STAIRS . . .
> ONE STEP AT A TIME.
>
> **- Joe Girard**

As you are likely aware, change is often hard for those involved. Many people resist change, whether it is small or large. This includes changing your own habits. Unfortunately, this resistance often stalls and often prevents the attainment of goals. But we have a simple behavior hack called "Quick Wins!" (Gavoni & Rodriguez, 2016).

A Quick Win is an improvement that is visible, has immediate benefit, and can be delivered quickly. The purpose is to create sustainability by engaging people. If it doesn't lead to sustainability, it wasn't a Quick Win. You see, people want to see meaningful improvement relatively quickly if they are going to remain engaged. In most cases, these improvements are easily identifiable and probably should have been made long ago. Quick Wins focus on getting people to engage in a couple of behaviors that, in the initial stages, require little effort but quickly result in a highly visible and meaningful change. Quick Wins are a good way to get buy-in and gain momentum as folks are more immediately rewarded for the effort.

In an organization, Quick Wins might be as simple as putting a new coat of paint in an area that looks dilapidated, improving the process for inputting time worked, or even something as simple as improving the process for calling out sick. Or it could be something as quick as getting input from employees on a change initiative and acting on it. Whatever it is, it requires little effort, it's highly visible to those involved, and it produces a meaningful outcome to the people involved.

In everyday life, fad diets have made a bundle off the concept at the root of Quick Wins. However, they weren't real Quick Wins because they weren't sustainable. For example, "Drink this diet shake for three days and you are guaranteed to lose five pounds." This excites you and increases the value of drinking the shakes (i.e., an establishing operation). So you do it. And with little effort, you quickly and visibly shed pounds. This is very meaningful! Soon you've ordered a year supply of the shakes, excited for the weight to melt off. But here's the thing: this meaningful outcome, dropping weight, was an illusion, as the shake was a diuretic that simply reduced your water weight. The weight you likely wanted to lose was fat. Not water! But seeing that weight drop increased your motivation to dig into your wallet and purchase more shakes. The problem is, it wasn't a Quick Win because it didn't lead to sustainability. If those who drank the shakes would have lost weight and this led to a healthy change in dietary habits, then it might be considered a Quick Win, as it got people moving in the right direction and kept them moving that way.

Quick Wins can be a powerful source of motivation. In everyday life, don't be afraid to grab the low-hanging fruit. If you taste it and it's good, you'll be more likely to climb the tree for more. Sometimes a Quick Win might just be getting a project started that you've been procrastinating on. Seeing the progress and getting that feeling of success is enough to prime your pump and keep you moving in the right direction. A good way to keep Quick Wins moving in the right direction when they are unable to see meaningful change for themselves is to provide people with graphic feedback. We'll discuss graphic feedback later in the book. But for now, know that it can help make the Quick Win salient or conspicuous to the person taking those small actions.

Behavior Hack #3 – Involve People

While a Quick Win does not have to be profound or have a long-term impact on your organization, it does require people to agree on the need for change, act together to make the change, and learn from the change. This means it's important to involve your people in goal setting. Provide them choices and give them a say. Nobody wants things done to them! For example, you likely don't want anybody telling you what goals you should be pursuing in your life. The goals you decide to pursue should be a function of what you value, not what others value. Similarly, involving people in goal setting in organizations is a great behavior hack for engaging them in work, as they've had a say in the process. The extent that people behave according to goals is drastically increased when they have helped to establish them. Consequently, they are more likely to continue performing effectively to achieve them. Similarly, in life, the extent people behave according to the goals they've established increases the likelihood they are living a meaningful life in their eyes (Hayes, 1993).

In fact, there is a concept that has been researched in behavior analysis called participatory management. Using this strategy, employees encourage their participation in the design and implementation of behavioral technology. By involving them in the creation and execution of simple strategies like prompting, self-reports, spot checks, and delivery of reinforcement, performance increased and was maintained for long periods of time. In one case, the researchers checked back five years later, and performance was still being maintained at high levels (Johnson, Welsh, Miller, & Altus, 1991).

In another research example, behavior analysts used a similar approach and found that the initial improvement in staff performance was maintained during their follow up assessment thirty years later!

Final Note

Involving people in goal setting and change initiatives, allowing them to make choices, and setting them free to pursue related accomplishments can be a powerful hack. In his book, *The Laws of Human Nature*, Robert Green explains that people need to feel autonomous. As such, involving people and providing choices are extremely powerful reinforcers, a concept that has been well researched (Martin, Yu, Martin, & Fazzio, 2006). This makes sense, given most people don't want to feel forced to do something. It's safe to say that when somebody has tried to force us to do something, it's not gone well. At a minimum, we've checked out. On the other end of that, we aren't ashamed to admit we've engaged in what is known in Applied Behavior Analysis (ABA) as *countercontrol*. *Countercontrol* refers to behavior that occurs in response to another's attempts to force somebody to do something (Delprato, 2002). And to be sure, this behavior is typically an attempt at punishing the person (well, actually the behavior) who is trying to force the response. You've likely been there, too. Perhaps somebody has yelled at you in order to get you to do something. You didn't like the way they approached you, so you yelled back. We don't blame you. This is a poor way to treat people, and a good way to generate lots of negative behavioral karma.

If you are like us and many others, when somebody attempts to force you to do something, or you feel like you're forced into a corner with no options, you will either check out, engage in countercontrol, dislike the person, or all three! So the simple behavior hack here is, provide choices by involving people in goal setting. This will increase the likelihood that they will engage in the behaviors required to achieve the goals.

We will talk more about punishment in chapter 7. As you move further into the book, we hope one thing is becoming progressively clearer. Success in life and leadership can be simplified into the arrangement of behavior and reinforcement that produce effective habits. Understanding some of the behavioral principles and hacks related to goal setting and attainment is critical to your success and is also part of the formula for deliberately spreading all sorts of positive behavioral karma!

KEY TAKEAWAYS:

- » Discover your aptitude.
- » Find your why.
- » Make your goals SMART.
- » Establish small goals.
- » Find Quick Wins.
- » Involve those you lead in goal setting.
- » Provide choices.

ASK YOURSELF:

- » What are you good at?
- » What are the people you lead good at?
- » What's important to you?
- » What's important to those you lead?
- » Where do you spend most of your free time?
- » Where do you find your mind drifting towards?
- » What are you doing when you feel at your best?
- » What are those you lead doing when they feel at their best?
- » What are you willing to try right now?
- » What are those you lead willing to try right now?
- » What can easily be achieved that is meaningful and visible?
- » Are you involving those you lead in setting goals?
- » Are you giving yourself the opportunity to have choices?
- » Are you providing choices to those you lead?

CHAPTER 7

Self-Monitoring and Report Out

To this point, we've talked about the importance of discovering your why, aligning behavior with results that move you or those you are leading toward those results, and setting motivational and attainable goals that serve as a source of measurement and reinforcement along your journey toward success. Now you must switch gears from planning the journey to not just monitoring progress toward your goal, but also the behaviors required to achieve it. In the '70s, *self-monitoring* became a term used to mean one's willingness to discriminate amongst social cues and respond accordingly under various conditions (Snyder, 1979). Since then, behavioral self-monitoring and reporting have been part of a packaged intervention that includes variables like goal setting and feedback as a practical approach to accelerate performance and achieve related outcomes in organizations (Olson & Winchester, 2008). For example, it has been used to improve interactions between staff and patients in an institution (Burgio, Whitman, & Reid, 1983), athletic performance (e.g., Kessler, 1985), academic performance (e.g., Dean, Malott, & Fulton, 1983), teacher performance (e.g., Browder, Liberty, Heller, & D'Huyvetters, 1986), safety performance (e.g., Ryan Olson & John Austin, 2001) and on-schedule and on-task performance in human services (Richman et al., 1988). The most common features related to behavioral self-monitoring and report out include instruction, materials for regular self-observing (e.g., paper checklist, iPad, wrist counters) within the natural environment, and dialogue with a supervisor regarding performance toward established goals (Olson & Winchester, 2008). Let's take a quick look at how we use self-monitoring and report out in our organization.

Self-Monitoring & Reporting Out for Accountability – Brett & Paulie's Story

> After pinpointing and goal setting, we then required each and every employee to keep a record of their hours worked that day and report it out to the leader of the division. Reporting out their hours worked and, moreover, seeing their numbers displayed on the graph that was texted to all employees, had an even bigger impact on increasing the hours worked. Employees saw how each of their work contributions helped the entire team meet their collective goal or fail to meet it. We witnessed more synergy, as evidenced by specific comments such as, "I babysat for Suzie so she could fulfill her hours, and it helped us meet our goal!" This teamwork began having an exponential compound effect.

As you can see from the above story, the process wasn't complex. It was simple. It has been our experience that complexity tends to be the enemy of improvement and scalability. Given the ease of implementing self-monitoring and report out procedures (e.g., checking a sheet and submitting the results to a supervisor with the understanding that it may be examined or audited by the supervisor for accuracy and future discussion), scaling and sustainability become increasingly achievable. This thought is supported by

Ludwig and Geller (2000) in their recommendations that the least intrusive process be used as primary interventions when seeking to impact performance and outcomes at scale. Incidentally, for those individuals who do not respond to these non-intrusive interventions, they recommend applying more intrusive interventions successively. For example, if self-monitoring was not proving to be effective, direct observation and feedback may be required if a performance deficit exists, or perhaps training if it is determined there is a skill deficit.

Some researchers have found self-monitoring and reporting to be unreliable in terms of the relation between the report and the actual behavior. Behavior analysts might call it a "say-do problem" (Geurin, & Foster, 1994) when individuals say they are doing this, but in actuality, they are doing something else. However, when self-monitoring and reporting were combined with immediate and continuous feedback, improvements in both accuracy of reports and performance were found across performers (Beal & Eubanks, 2008). Moreover, self-monitoring has also demonstrated potency in improving performance across organizations. For example, in one study (Richman, Riordan, Reiss, Pyles, & Bailey, 1988), employees carried individual cards where they self-monitored and recorded their on-schedule and on-task performance. At the end of each day, they handed their cards to their supervisors, who intermittently provided immediate feedback based on the data recorded. Under these conditions, performance improved more than 50 percent!

When somebody is asked to record aspects of his or her behavior, simply engaging in the recording process is an antecedent that serves as a prompt regarding the behavioral expectations. In other words, just getting into the habit of looking at the recording form just prior to engaging in a specific task increases the likelihood it will be completed successfully, especially if the form is task analyzed. And if one completes the task successfully, this increases the likelihood of reinforcement and the development of habit-strength behavior. Furthermore, the expectations of recording a behavior may also increase the likelihood the recorder will need to measure the behavior more precisely in order to record it. This has the added benefit of refining performance.

Sometimes self-monitoring can function as a positively or negatively reinforcing consequence depending on how an individual rates him or herself. High scores may serve to increase the likelihood they will engage in the behaviors that led to such a score (Malott, R., Malott, M., & Trojan, E., 1999). In contrast, self-reporting a low score may serve as a negative reinforcer, resulting in the reporter increasing response effort (i.e., trying harder!) to avoid recording the lower number. For example, escape or avoidance behaviors like loafing or other behaviors disassociated with the targeted behaviors and related outcomes might be replaced with other alternative or even incompatible behaviors that will produce better outcomes. We will return to self-monitoring and report outs in an organization. But let's look at why and how it is important to helping you achieve more in any area of your life.

We Must Be Aware

Whatever set of complex behavioral mechanisms are at play (Olson & Austin, 2001), self-monitoring and reporting out is a simple and easy-to-implement process that can result in improved behavior and outcomes. And all of this self-monitoring talk applies to you too. As a leader of your life or others, it is important you monitor yourself. You must be aware! As such, you must learn to be a good observer of your behavior, the behavior of others, the impact of your behavior on your environment, and the impact of the environment on your behavior. In turn, as a leader of others, you must help them do the same. Remember, people are part of your environment, and you are part of theirs. As a stream of data being fed to a CPU, this reciprocal feedback acts as a kind of loop that either maintains behavior, increases it or decreases it based on the consequences that occur as a result. More on this later in the feedback chapter. For now, you might think about self-monitoring as a means of gathering your own feedback from the environment, so you can act accordingly and help others to do the same.

Unfortunately, most people tend to be poor observers of their behavior and the impact of it. This includes their internal (i.e., covert) behavior, their private thoughts, feelings, and sensations. People also tend to be very poor observers of the purpose or function of their behavior or their more immediate why. As such, they often behave in ways that result in the most immediate reinforcing consequence, even if it derails them from more important longer-term goals. Remember, whether something is added or subtracted as a result of their behavior, if this consequence is reinforcing, the behavior will occur again, and again, and again. Eventually, habits are formed, and oftentimes folks (this includes us!) can't even remember why they began engaging in the behavior in the first place. "It's just the way I do things." In an organization, behavior consistently applied across employees becomes what is known as culture, or "the way we do things around here." If this is productive and valued behavior that leads to meaningful outcomes, it's probably a good thing. If it's not, it can be bad, very bad. The collective behaviors of you or those within your organization can lead to the development of internal behaviors that serve as obstacles to the achievement of goals. We are sure you are familiar with these behaviors like fear, anxiety, and a variety of other self-defeating thoughts, feelings, and bodily sensations that just plain don't feel good.

Now, a few of you might be thinking, "Those aren't behaviors." Unfortunately, that's a misnomer and one that has certainly played a major part in preventing ABA from being the go-to for helping all people overcome both behavioral and mental health issues. We don't want to stray off topic too much, but it's important to visit this concept, as it's pertinent to recognizing and overcoming internal obstacles like anxiety and self-defeating thoughts to achieve goals. You see, most people think that behaviorism focuses exclusively on what people do. In other words, their actions or the things we can all see. For most people outside of the behavior analytic community, behaviorism appears to be a philosophy that is too simplistic, as they believe it relates only to behavior that can be seen while denying the presence of thinking and importance of genetic predisposition (Skinner, 1974). For most of you reading this who aren't behavior analysts, here is some surprising news: Behaviorism doesn't discount private events like thoughts and feelings. Rather, private events are recognized as covert behavior that only the person can observe (Moore, 2001). For instance, we can't observe what you are thinking, but you can! So essentially, when you hear about mental health, what is being talked about is behavioral health. We really look forward to the future when we are likely able to measure covert behavior with the right neurological technology, so we can consider isolating thoughts as potential independent variables or having possible causal effects.

Many mental health researchers and experts suggest organizations promote well-being through mindfulness as a means of increasing productivity and success (e.g., Slade, 2010; Hyland & Mills, 2015; Janssen et al., 2018; Hayes et al., 2019). We should note, promoting well-being means engaging in behaviors that reinforce habits associated with being well! It's not unusual to find common recommendations like:

- Track and reflect on daily behaviors (habit)
- Link habits to unproductive emotional responses like anxiety (linking behavior to results)
- Develop productive behavioral responses (habits) like engagement in class
- Make the process intentional and strategic (focusing on pinpointed behaviors that lead to desired results)

So essentially, what these experts are recommending for improving mental health and outcomes through mindfulness approaches is for employees to develop good habits and be mindful of the associated behaviors. Given this all focuses on behavior, you can see why we believe a better term, in this case, might be *behavioral health*, not *mental health*.

Self-Monitoring & Report Out – Brett's Story

Another very practical application of self-monitoring and reporting out for accountability has been extremely effective with my stepson for completing chores. He sets the alarm on his phone each day that reminds him of his five chores and is required to text me that they are completed (or not completed) every day by 9:00 p.m. Initially, he was only required to do the jobs and not text the results to me, and his performance was poor. After he was required to text the results to me, we saw tremendous improvement in chore completion. One factor that may have contributed to the success of this self-monitoring and report out procedure was that he received zero credit if he could not remember to send the text (even if the chore was completed). I speculate the program has been successful because he knows a permanent product (or work accomplishment) is always present on my text threads for me to go back and review and audit his performance. My stepson has reported that it was his idea to set the alarm as a reminder to send the text because he wanted to make sure he was always credited for the work by remembering to leave the permanent product accomplishment of a text message.

Unfortunately, whether it be covert or overt, sometimes it's like we have blinders on that too often impact our objectivity when it comes to behavior. For example, most children behave exceptionally well at school. However, it's misbehavior that tends to enlist the most frequent and immediate attention in lieu of prosocial and other behavior suitable to the context. What's funny is that it seems to work in reverse when we evaluate ourselves. Many times, our errant behavior goes unrecognized, with most of our attention directed toward the exceptional behavior we engage in. In a way, we are all very biased regarding our own covert and overt behavior, as we tend to more frequently recognize or confirm only select behaviors and the impact of them, and discount or deny others. It's like a coach who favors certain players but only notices the others when their performance is poor. This confirmation bias acts as a reinforcing feedback loop that increases and strengthens our thoughts and actions. Oh, to be an objective observer of behavior, especially our own! How different things might be if only we could all truly recognize and determine the impact of our behavior on others—and ourselves.

Not our intent. Our impact. What would it be like to understand how we are perceived through the eyes of others, and how does that contrast with how we perceive ourselves and our own impact?

So how can we do this? How can we determine SMART pinpoints and then commit to behaving in ways that help us reach our goals, even in the presence of crappy thoughts and feelings? Well, thankfully, a growing body of research behind acceptance and commitment therapy or training (ACT) (Strosahl, Hayes, Wilson, & Gifford, 2004) can help us improve self-control. You remember self-control. This is when we choose a larger delayed consequence (like losing weight) over a smaller, more immediate one (like eating a cookie) in order to achieve outcomes. ACT helps move us toward who and what we value. It can accelerate the attainment of goals while simultaneously reducing unhealthy and self-defeating thoughts (i.e., covert behavior) and the resulting overt behavior or actions that tend to move us away from our values.

While the behavioral science underpinning ACT can get very deep, we want to provide you with just enough information to help you understand the basics and better apply the concepts. ACT is an effective and evidence-based approach rooted in overcoming inner obstacles (e.g., self-doubt, fear, anxiety) to achieve personal or organizational goals and lead a happier and more productive personal and professional life. One might think of it as the science of mindfulness. Because of its simplicity, it is our contention that the ACT matrix illustrated below (fig. 10) is a behavior hack that can be used at scale to support productivity and increase positive behavioral karma across individuals, families, groups, and organizations. While ACT has typically been applied to support the improvement of mental health issues, the approach easily can be applied to the work setting given contingencies (remember, think: If I do this, then this will occur) as they relate to goals by helping shift our attention to the longer-term implications of actions (Atkins, Wilson, Hayes, 2019). If a worker values achieving a goal, they will be more likely to both learn and engage in the performance that will lead them toward it (Bond, Hayes, & Barnes-Homes, 2006).

A practical and concrete method, the ACT matrix (Polk, Schoendorff, Webster, Olaz, 2016) can serve as a self-monitoring tool to help you better discriminate or notice covert behaviors within your skin (i.e., private events that only you can observe like thoughts) and overt behaviors outside the skin (i.e., what other people can observe, or your actions). As a result, you can also better understand the function of your behavior (i.e., why you do certain things), how those behaviors impact you and others, and how to identify behaviors that move you toward who and what you value. Once you are able to recognize and sort these behaviors into the appropriate bucket, you then must become an ACTer as you actively engage in the development of habits required to achieve valued outcomes.

A Tour of the ACT Matrix

The matrix (fig. 10), a blank one of which is located in the appendix, consists of four quadrants. These quadrants allow you to sort behaviors (i.e., overt behaviors that you can be observed doing), values, and private events (i.e., covert behaviors like thoughts, feelings, bodily sensations that only you can observe).

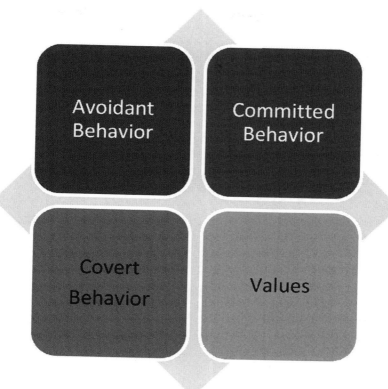

Figure 10: ACT matrix

Values

To begin, use the blank matrix we've included in the appendix. In the lower right quadrant, list who and what you value. Values are not destinations or achievements, but rather guiding principles that help us to choose meaningful actions. The easiest way to start thinking about values is to think of who and what is important to you. While you are certainly important to yourself, you probably have a variety of family, friends, or colleagues who are also important to you, people you value caring for and connecting with. Or perhaps it's something to do with a role that allows you to be useful or helpful to others, a recreation that allows you to be physically active, caring for your body, which allows you to be healthy. Or perhaps it is your purpose or why, as we discussed in the last chapter that drives your learning or allows you to better understand yourself.

When it comes to setting short and long-term goals, you must first have a clear understanding of your values. Goals are not values, as they are concrete things that can be accomplished. But goals should be driven by your values. These might be related to areas like your purpose, roles, recreation, health, or perhaps relationships. If you value spending time with your partner, for example, then perhaps a short-term goal might be to travel to different places within your state with them each month, with a long-term goal of traveling out of the state with them at least once each year. The driver of those goals is clearly the value of time spent with your partner.

Covert Behavior

In the lower-left quadrant, you would list private events, or covert behaviors, such as thoughts (e.g., "I can't do this"), feelings (e.g., "I'm anxious"), bodily sensations (e.g., "I have butterflies in my stomach"), etc. that might show up and prevent you from moving toward who and what you value and prevent you from achieving your goals. Remember, these are still behaviors, but they are covert, as they are those behaviors that only you can observe. All of the crummy thoughts, feelings, and bodily sensations that show up inside of you can't be observed by others. But they are very real to you. And they can often get in the way of reaching your goals as fatigue, anger, anxiety, or negative thoughts such as, "I can't do this," thereby impacting what you do in your day-to-day life. Consequently, these covert behaviors can be good predictors of unproductive behavior.

In fact, our covert behaviors may be far more powerful than we know in terms of their impact on our environment. In theories posited by quantum mechanics, a big mystery is the fact that the outcome of a quantum experiment can change depending on whether or not the experimenter chooses to measure some property of the particles involved. In the world of behavior analysis, this might be known as *observer reactivity*. In essence, this would suggest that in some way, our environment behaves based on how we look at it. To some, this might appear mystical. And maybe it is; however, it might be worth taking a look at through a lens rooted in the science of human behavior since it is behavior that might be at work!

Avoidant Behavior

In the upper left quadrant, you would list what overt behaviors lead you away from the people and things you value or prevent you from reaching goals. Oftentimes people might be unaware of these behaviors and negative behavioral karma being created. But they engage in them because they work in one way or another. And while they are productive in the sense that they can provide some sort of immediate relief, and sometimes this is okay, they often can be unproductive, as they can also be simultaneously moving you away from your values. These behaviors might be considered avoidant, as they temporarily allow people to avoid or escape the crummy thoughts and feelings that show up at the expense of moving toward what's most valued. Think about how it feels to move away from negative thoughts, anxiety, or anger. If your overt behaviors or actions are successful, then they likely result in a sense of relief.

The sense of relief produced by these actions serves as a negative reinforcer (i.e., it subtracts something aversive) and will increase the likelihood you will behave this way again. We all behave in ways that allow us to escape things that may be undesirable. The problem is, sometimes these behaviors are simultaneously moving us away from who and what we value and often prevent us from reaching our goals. While they do provide us immediate relief, it tends to be only temporary. For example, in a relationship when two people argue, it might be that one is angry at the other for speaking to them a certain way. As a result, they respond with anger in attempts to avoid being spoken to that way again in the future. Drinking alcohol, in some cases, is another example when somebody is doing it to temporarily avoid a bad feeling. For example, in the opening story about Brett, he increased his alcohol frequency to escape all the bad thoughts and feelings (covert behaviors) associated with the lengthy divorce proceedings. His behavior did serve to provide him a sense of immediate gratification. But each time he engaged in drinking and other unproductive behavior, it chipped away at what was most important to him: his family.

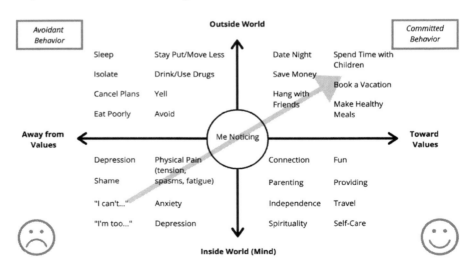

Figure 11: ACT Matrix Illustration

Unfortunately, some folks get caught in a vicious cycle as the *away* behaviors (drinking) further exacerbate our crummy thoughts, feelings, and sensations, as drinking likely hasn't moved them closer to established goals. While these behaviors may have started off as a fun escape from stress, they become habitual for some and wind up having a profound and negative behavioral karma effect on their lives and the lives of those around them.

Committed Behavior

Remember, nothing is achieved without behavior. If you want to overcome all the bad thoughts and feelings and refrain from doing things that make your life worse, you must do something else, or what we might call *replacement behaviors*. In the upper right quadrant, you would list or pinpoint what behaviors will lead you toward the people and things you value. Imagine not seeing your child or significant other for a long time. You miss them, dearly. Now think about how it feels to literally move toward them—literally, how it would feel to walk toward your child or significant other for the first time after a long absence. You probably would feel a sense of benevolence or well-being. If you've done a good job determining a few SMART pinpoints that will lead to your goals as we've discussed in Chapters 3 & 4, these can be listed in this section.

As you know, you can't get to where you are going unless you first know how to get there. Researchers spend a lifetime trying to predict the reliable impact of independent variables upon dependent variables. Fortunately, in personal and professional life, there is a ton of literature that now exists and tells us exactly what behavior we need to commit to that will move us from here to there. There is no need to guess and experience negative consequences that might be associated with trial and error—for example, this book. So make sure you do your homework so you can determine the most effective and efficient behaviors to engage in. But while knowing the right thing to do is an important piece of the formula for success, you must also avoid the pitfalls and "hooks" that tend to keep people stuck in a rut. To do this, you must remain psychologically flexible.

Psychological Flexibility

Psychological flexibility can be thought of as being aware or *mindful* of one's behavior and the environment *in the present moment,* and then doing the right thing at the right time across contexts, regardless of the negative thoughts, feelings, or bodily sensations they might be experiencing (Hayes, Strosahl, Bunting, Twohig, & Wilson, 2004). In the most basic of terms that relate to our book, it's being an objective observer or *noticing* your behavior (this includes both overt and covert behavior) in the context of the current conditions, and then self-initiating and engaging in the valued behaviors you've pinpointed that will lead you to your value-driven goals under those conditions. Even in the presence of crummy thoughts and feelings, we feel you can accomplish anything when effectively taking actions that are aligned with your values, as long as you aren't attempting to focus on too many objectives. Unfortunately, most of us tend to overthink things or get stuck on them, especially when we have bad thoughts and feelings. We try to rationalize these thoughts and feelings to help us feel better (Hayes et al., 1996). We actually set up impossible rules for ourselves that become habitual and prevent us from actively engaging in productive behavior. This rule-governed behavior, as we discussed in chapter 2, wastes precious time and energy that would be better served engaging in the behaviors that will lead us toward the who and what that will truly make us feel better.

For example, as budding combat athletes, we used to spend precious time and energy worrying if we'd perform well and win. We might then start to get that sick feeling in our stomach as we began to think negative thoughts like, "My upcoming opponent is better than me," or, "I'm feeling a little sluggish today. I'm going to lose!" We were stuck! As a result, we then might spend precious energy trying to tell ourselves that we shouldn't be feeling this way. We then might talk to a bunch of peers or coaches hoping they might say just the right thing to help us get rid of that crummy feeling and help us feel better. While the crummy feeling may have gone away, it was always only very temporary. And all that time and energy was wasted. What we should have done was focused on engaging in the actual pinpointed behaviors that would increase the likelihood of performing well and getting our hand raised through training! It's imperative to focus on and commit to engaging in behaviors that lead you to what you want as opposed to getting stuck in all the mud of negative thoughts and feelings related to what you don't want and then engaging in behaviors to avoid the bad stuff. While it might provide temporary relief, it simultaneously moves you away from your values.

Another example that might be recognizable to most people can be found in music. Some songs make us feel wonderful. We can listen to them over and over again because they evoke a positive feeling or memory. Unfortunately, in contrast to a song that makes you reminisce about a meaningful moment or time in your life when you hear it on the radio, there are also the songs that evoke a negative feeling or make you relive a moment you wish never occurred. All of those bad feelings rush through you as soon as you hear that first note—in this case, that first thought. Instead of being made up of notes, it's made up of words. And then as a rule, if you purposely avoid listening to channels that play the said song, the very act of trying to avoid the song evokes those feelings. It's truly a vicious cycle as we end up developing habits that involve engaging in unproductive behaviors that temporarily allow us to get rid of, or at least minimize, unwanted thoughts and feelings. This type of inflexible response typically does not move us toward our goals.

When you are aware of your vulnerabilities and accept your undesirable thoughts and feelings and instead without perseverating on the negative, commit to behaviors that lead you to who or what you value, you will move toward value-driven goals and experience a sense of satisfaction as you do. Through systematic repetition of exposure to the crummy covert behaviors and noticeable movement toward your values (i.e., reinforcers), you eventually become desensitized as the bad stuff gets smaller and smaller and negative thoughts, feelings, and behaviors are replaced with positive ones. The ripple effect of positive behavioral karma takes over as the goodness you experience becomes multiplied as the result of your productive habits.

> *SHORT-TERM GAIN = LONG-TERM GAIN*
>
> *SHORT-TERM PAIN = LONG-TERM GAIN*

In an earlier example, we discussed our fear of public speaking, one that is not uncommon to most folks. But we remained psychologically flexible and essentially carried the baggage with us. Like jumping in a cold pool without thinking about it, we just dove in and did it, regardless of the anxiety we were experiencing. The result: massive doses of reinforcement in the form of meaningful experiences with participants, networking, disseminating the science, and many other things. The positive behavioral karma we've experienced because of it is immeasurable. From meeting and collaborating with amazing people to being provided with various opportunities that aligned with our values, these positive outcomes would have never occurred and multiplied had we not noticed and accepted the bad inside stuff, linked it to unproductive behaviors that moved us away from what we valued, and then relentlessly committed to the behaviors that would move us in the right direction.

Whether you are trying to accomplish a goal in your life, or reach goals established in your organization, using the ACT matrix can allow you to better discriminate and sort your private events (covert behaviors), unproductive behaviors, and pinpointed behaviors that if you commit to will lead you to desired results. And here is the great thing about the ACT matrix: it can be easily used at the organizational level by having groups identify common values, common private events that show up and get in the way of moving toward those values, common unproductive behaviors, and the critical behaviors required to move toward the common values. When people share values, it leads to a shared identity, motivation, cooperation, and accomplishment (Atkins, Wilson, Hayes, 2019). Let's take a look at a couple of hacks for effectively using ACT in life and leadership.

Hacking ACT

Sometimes half the battle is just recognizing or helping others recognize; they are hooked in a vicious and unproductive cycle related to thoughts and behaviors. Like a positive impulse, the simple act of being aware that we are engaging in these behaviors can serve to prompt a pinpointed or committed behavior. It's not that we don't want to do the right thing; it's that we just aren't in the habit because we haven't gotten in touch with enough reinforcement. If we are able to notice we are engaging in unproductive thoughts or behaviors, it can actually serve as an *impulse* or prompt that reminds us of the behaviors we're committed to. Unlike impulsive behavior characterized by engaging in behavior first and thinking about the consequences after, we characterize this as a *positive impulse* because the valued results and critical behaviors have already been identified. Let's take a look at the *5-second rule* (Robbins, 2017), a very cool behavior hack for using the recognition of unproductive thoughts and feelings as a positive impulse that can increase psychological flexibility to generate committed behavior, which leads to the achievement of goals.

The 5 Second Rule – Paulie's Story

"Five . . . six . . ." The Teco Arena is packed as seven thousand screaming fans roar with delight and hundreds of thousands watching at home salivate in anticipation as they watch the most viewed show on FX. At that moment, the roar seems like distant thunder as the lights hanging from the massive dome ceiling begin to come into focus. "What the hell am I doing down here?" I ask myself. The realization quickly hits me like

a hammer. I'm in a fight. It's spring 2002. At 201 pounds, 6'0",
I've entered the Toughman Tournament as the smallest fighter
in the heavyweight division. It's my second fight of the night,
and third within the past two days. My opponent, 6'3", 285
pounds, stares down at me from the neutral corner having
just dropped me with a glancing overhand right. It was the first
punch he connected. "Seven . . . Eight . . ." the referee bellows
as he stands over me, arms shooting toward the ceiling in
regular intervals while he counts. "Nine . . ." And I'm up. "There's
no way I'm going out like this," I tell myself. "I'm going out on my
shield," flashes through my mind, and old warrior maxim that
essentially means "I'll go down fighting."

The ref uses his shirt to dust off my gloves and signals for the
fight to resume. My opponent closes the distance to finish
what he started, a knowing look in his eye. We both know that
if he lands another punch like that, I won't be getting up. As he
steps within proximity, he launches the same right hand that
dropped me. But this time, I see it coming and manage to roll
under it, where I find myself in a very familiar position. In fact,
it's my favorite position. A position that allows me to unleash
the most powerful weapon in my personal arsenal. The left
hook to the body, a.k.a., the liver shot. And as luck would have
it, my opponent has left his body exposed. So I shoot my best
Sunday punch . . . and land. My opponent quivers briefly and
then collapses to his knees in pain, unable to get up by the
tenth count. The crowd goes absolutely bonkers as the referee
raises my hand in victory. I've done it. I've won. And I don't mean
the fight. I mean, I've beat myself. I've overcome my own fear.
There's an old martial art saying I have tattooed on my back

that says, "True victory is victory over oneself," a principle I live by as I try to be better tomorrow than I am today.

You see, my rational self, my intellectual self, wouldn't have gotten up. I'm no fool, and though the name of the tournament is the Toughman, I don't consider myself the stereotypical tough guy. I just enjoy challenging myself. I mean, this guy dropped me with his first punch. If I had time to think about it, I probably would have determined I was waaaaay over my head and thought I should've never entered this tournament, at least not as a damn heavyweight! But in those five seconds that I came awake, there was no time for those self-defeating thoughts. I needed to act. Not think, *act*. And by doing so, I put myself in a position to achieve victory. Had I not, had I thought and decided to allow the ref to count to ten, I may have lived in regret and maybe even become consumed with the feeling that I was a quitter who does not live up to his own principles.

So what's the point of this story? As we discussed, people get hooked on unwanted thoughts and feelings. When they do, they behave in ways that allow them to escape and then avoid them in the future. Once they accept the thoughts and feelings and recognize the behaviors that get in the way, they still must act. This is where people fall short. Well, we've got a powerful behavior hack for you. It's called the *5-second rule*. And just like it worked in the fight illustrated above, it can work for you to overcome self-defeating thoughts and then self-initiate and engage in behaviors that will move toward who and what and achieve even your biggest goals.

According to Mel Robbins, Author of The 5 Second Rule (2017), it works like this: if you have an impulse to act on a value-driven goal, you must physically move within 5 seconds, or your brain will kill the idea using your automated rule-governed behavior. Essentially, while knowing what you value and identifying the behaviors you should engage in is essential for reaching goals, it's insufficient. You *must* act. And where being impulsive tends to be framed negatively, in this case, it's a positive thing, as the impulse is aligned with established goals and the pinpointed behaviors that will lead you to them.

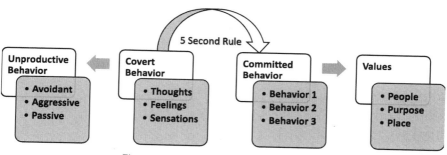

Figure 12: 5 Second Rule Illustration

We use it, and it works. We both have a goal of making it to the gym or exercising at least three days a week. As a result of combining ACT with the 5-second rule, we've both been smashing that goal. Here's how it works for us. In the past, when we were finished working, we might sit down in front of the TV, listen to music, or tend to some other business. Then a thought would shoot through our head like lightning: "You should work out." The past us might seriously consider it and then determine that we're too tired or busy and then tell ourselves that we'll make up for it later in the week. We talk ourselves right out of it, and of course, we don't hit our goal of making it to the gym three days a week. But now, as soon as the thought shoots through our mind after work, we stand up and engage in the first of a chain of behaviors that will lead us to exercise or head to the gym. For example, we might grab our socks and shoes and put them on the ground in front of the couch. This is like *behavioral momentum,* which entails making relatively easier requests before presenting requests that are more challenging or difficult (Craig, Nevin, & Odum, 2014). This easy-to-engage-in behavior moves us in the right direction, and soon we are dressed and heading to work out.

So, if you want to reach goals and live a more productive life, you must determine your goals based on your values, align critical behaviors, and then act. Don't think, act. And when possible, do it in five seconds. The trick is to engage in a behavior. Even the smallest action can prime the pump, so to speak, and get you going and keep you moving in the right direction.

Self-Monitoring and Report Out ACT at the Organizational Level

Many people rise to leadership positions based on their ability to perform well. As a leader, they seek to reproduce and scale their success to achieve goals that lead to valued business outcomes. Unfortunately, it is not uncommon for new leaders to make the fatal assumption that, "If you understand the technical work of a business, you understand a business that does that technical work" (Gerber, 1995). In other words, just because you are a solid practitioner in a particular field does not mean you will be able to influence the behavior of others as a leader. Influencing the behavior of others is a different skill set. And it is rooted in behavioral principles, many of which you have been reading about up to this point. Beyond understanding the principles of behavior, many leaders must acquire technical skill sets related to the nature of their industry and their leadership position within an organization. For example, possessing a fundamental understanding of issues related to human resources and having to deal with taxes and basic accounting. If these leaders are going to move an organization toward valued outcomes, they must know exactly what behaviors to commit to. There is a lot to learn.

Like the old saying goes, what gets measured gets done. As such, one area that an organizational leader must become familiar with to be able to notice if the folks within the organization are collectively moving toward valued outcomes is the use of *key performance indicators* (KPIs) and reporting out. A KPI is simply a critical (key) indicator of progress toward a pinpointed result. Just like people notice measurable differences during self-monitoring, organizations use KPIs to evaluate their movement towards reaching targeted goals. And just like pinpointing the right behaviors to commit to is the result of pinpointing a very clear and precise desired result, pinpointing the right KPI as a measure of movement toward value-driven goals depends on both the industry and which part of the business is desired to be tracked given that each department will have KPIs specific to their goals. Once these KPIs are pinpointed, they can then be input into a data dashboard and a graphic display regularly used by departments as a self-monitoring tool that can also be reported out to senior leadership and used to track progress and respond with agility.

For example, an organization might value providing quality mentoring to their staff, as they believe this impacts many business results, like employee satisfaction, customer satisfaction, retention, and revenue. As such, a KPI might be the number of feedback surveys that reach a targeted goal (e.g., 4.5 in the graph example [fig. 13]) and fall below a certain rating (e.g., 4 in the graph example [fig. 13]) on their scale. By monitoring this, the department which oversees the mentoring program is able to measure (i.e., self-monitor) how well they are meeting the goal of providing quality mentoring and then report this to the CEO. The achievement of goals can be met with pay for performance, which we will discuss later. And if they aren't meeting these goals, they then take a deeper look using the 5 laws, take action, and then continue to self-monitor and report out until the goal is met. Check out this real-life example below (fig. 13) from our division in Maine related to the employees' satisfaction with their job and their mentor. Around November and December, the team observed a drop in satisfaction and took action. As a result of applying the 5 laws, you will note the remarkable increasing and sustainable trend, even in the midst of the coronavirus crisis.

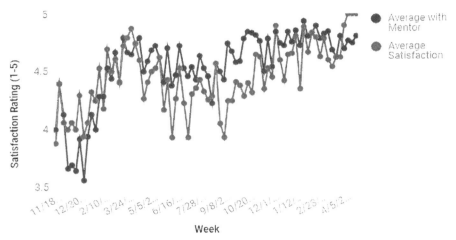

Figure 13: Satisfaction survey data

While this might seem overly simple, it is critical to get it right, as pinpointing the wrong KPI can paint an inaccurate picture that generates inefficient, ineffective, and costly responses as the result of the unproductive behavior it generates. For example, in the illustration above (fig. 13), if the organization only looked at raw numbers of surveys that fell below a 4 without considering their rapid growth, it might indicate a greater number of people are dissatisfied. However, when considering the number of 4s in relation to the number of employees, this data might actually demonstrate improved satisfaction. Can you imagine the chain of time-consuming and costly actions that might occur as a result of this analysis?

Developing KPIs doesn't have to be complicated. Here is a simple behavior hack laid out in a procedure that might help you more efficiently get it done by taking advantage of simple technology and dividing and conquering.

1. Using an Excel spreadsheet, targeted individuals enter data.
2. KPI data is summarized in a graph and entered into a slide for easy visual analysis. For example, graphs that reflect:
   a) Revenue
   b) Payroll
   c) Compliance
   d) Utilization
5. Hold virtual meetings (this saves time) where the KPI slide deck is the focus of the meeting. As part of the meeting:
   a) A quick check-in to see how things are going.
   b) Review of each KPI.

Pinpointing and using KPIs to maximize performance and profit is critical to the success of any organization. The process, as illustrated above, does not have to be complicated; however, it has to be consistent, the KPIs need to be precise, and data should be used to project, problem-solve, and reinforce, not punish! Some things to consider when determining your KPIs include the following:

- Which metrics align with the mission?
- How many should you have? (Be careful of paralysis through analysis!)
- What measures are leading indicators?
- What measures are lagging indicators?

- How often should you measure?
- How often should the metrics be shared?
- Which metrics should be shared with which stakeholders?
- Who will input the data?
- Who will share the metrics with stakeholders (in graph form, preferably)?
- What are the important subgoals and goals?

ACTing to Accomplish KPIs, Connecting Behavior with Valued Results

KPIs can be used at different levels and across different departments within an organization as a means of self-monitoring and reporting out to improving performance, climate, culture, and the achievement of goals. A nice behavior hack for engaging employees in their work is to shift job descriptions and scorecards for bonuses and raises from results to accomplishments or work outputs (Binder, 1998), like the number of decisions, deliverables, relationships, transactions, milestones, etc. that are the products of behavior in the workplace. As Binder (2009) reminds us, these accomplishments or work outputs describe "what the organization needs from its people," as they link the actions of people to valued results. Much like a GPS, accomplishments do a better job of letting both leadership and the performer know they are moving in the right direction, as measuring long-term business results can be *demotivating* because they are too delayed from our day-to-day hard work. Sometimes this can result in feelings of apathy, anxiety, or any variety of negative thoughts and feelings that lead to unproductive behaviors. Remember, sometimes private events and related unproductive behaviors can be predicted and planned for, even in an organization. For example, if you can predict resistance to change will lead to unproductive behaviors because you've heard people grumbling "this will never work," you might share stories of a similar change working in another organization, share data on the success, and engage in Quick Wins to gain momentum and buy-in. Oftentimes these Quick Wins can come in the form of accomplishments.

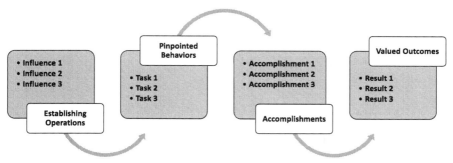

Figure 14: Accomplishments as Measures of Progress

Accomplishments are what people must do in order to help the organization achieve valued outcomes. As such, measuring accomplishments can be extremely motivating because, because like a Quick Win, they often produce immediate, visible, permanent products of our day-to-day behavior. Accomplishments strengthen and sustain behavior by acting as both a conditioned or naturally occurring reinforcer as performers observe themselves moving in a valued direction. And of course, this puts leadership in the position to reinforce the performer, thus strengthening performance.

Behavior Hacks for Self-Monitoring Your Leadership

As we discussed in section 1, leadership is a very important concept. Whether it be leading a household, team, classroom, organization, state, or even country, leadership has the potential to make or break. A group or organization without a leader is much like a ship without

BRETT DINOVI & PAUL GAVONI

a captain. Unfortunately, good leadership is hard to find. Why? Well, we believe part of the reason is that people think leadership is an inherent quality that only a few fortunate are born with. They don't see themselves as somebody who has the "right stuff," so to speak. As a result, too many leadership positions are filled with people who have the "wrong stuff" or those who seek out leadership positions for the purpose of adding value to their own lives, not the lives of the people they are leading. Like the old saying goes, if people aren't following, you aren't leading. You're just a guy or gal out, taking a walk.

Unfortunately, some leaders are very influential in the wrong way. They use coercive behaviors to ensure people are getting the job done. Privately, we call these types of behaviors *shitty leadership*. Unfortunately, many folks don't recognize their shitty leadership. There is a disconnect between their perception of themselves and the perception of their "followers." They think, "I'm not that guy (or gal)." And we hope *you* aren't that guy or gal either, but it's possible. If you want to find out, we have a hack in the form of a simple self-assessment through the usage of the tips outlined below. If, as a result of this quick assessment, you discover you are providing shitty leadership, don't think of yourself as a bad person. You behave this way because it works—well, at least from your perspective. But there is another way, and it's a better way. It's important for anybody who aspires to be an effective leader to have a fundamental understanding of the 5 laws and behavioral karma so they can achieve discretionary effort from those they are leading. This includes you!

As we mentioned, people with shitty leadership behavior typically don't think they are behaving "shittily." If you were to ask them, "Are you being shitty?" They would say, "No way! I know better than that," and then would quickly rationalize their behavior. However, their employees would say otherwise. This lack of awareness or noticing their own unproductive behavior and the long-term impact of their behaviors in terms of moving toward their values is often the culprit. You remember these behaviors, the ones identified in the top left corner of the ACT matrix. These leaders do what they do because they think it works—and it does if all they want is compliance and they don't value the ethical treatment of people. The solution? In short, leaders need to be more observant of their behavior and how it impacts others. We'll talk more about increasing the ability for leaders to self-monitor through reciprocal feedback and leadership assessments like 360-degree surveys in the next chapter. For now, we want to share eight quick signs you can use to assess if you or somebody you know is engaged in shitty leadership behavior. If you are displaying any of these shitty behaviors, you may want to do a deeper self-assessment:

Sign 1: You regularly blame people first rather than look at the environmental contingencies (including your behavior) that support their performance. Listen, it's easy to blame so-and-so for not doing their job, but blame does not get down to the root of the issue. It's like a coach blaming the team for failing. Sometimes the coach needs to look in the mirror.

Sign 2: You always feel like you need to be present to make sure the job gets done right. If you constantly find yourself thinking or saying, "When you want the job done right, you have to do it yourself," you may want to take a look at yourself. You may justify this by seeing yourself a perfectionist. Well, perhaps, but it might also be that your leadership behavior is shitty.

Sign 3: If you feel like you have all the answers and regularly fail to solicit input from your followers, your leadership might be shitty. At meetings, these types of leaders regularly make a bunch of demands but ask for very little input from people.

Sign 4: You focus more on the task and result and less on the people. If you find yourself only thinking about getting the job done and not thinking about the people required to do it, your leadership might be shitty. Good leaders are tapped into the values of their people and regularly make an effort to tie in their day-to-day work with valued outcomes.

Sign 5: You have a group of followers who regularly report on the shortcomings of other members of the group or organization. Akin to tattlers in elementary school, or corporate spies, if you will, these folks are provided ample reinforcement through your responses. If you have more people tattling than those providing positive feedback, your leadership might be shitty.

Sign 6: When people make mistakes, they rarely tell you because you'll likely lash out at them. And when they do, it's typically because they know you will find out. Effective leaders provide a safety net for people, one where folks feel comfortable to admit and learn from a mistake, and regularly seek the leader out for advice. If people rarely admit mistakes or frequently blame others, your leadership might be shitty.

Sign 7: If you regularly demean people in front of others and you rationalize it as a lesson to them and others, your leadership is definitely shitty. If telling people what to do and demeaning them created lasting success, there would be many more highly successful leaders and organizations. This is not the way—ever!

Sign 8: You treat people differently based on their position on the org chart. This one drives us nuts! Everybody, we mean *everybody* should be treated with the same respect. If you are more friendly to those higher up the org chart than you are to those below you, well, Houston, we have a problem.

Sign 9: If you can't motivate people to do something you've requested them to do, you fear doing it yourself and fail to roll up your shirt sleeves and just do it.

Listen, if you regularly display one or any combination of these behaviors, don't be disheartened. It's your behavior, not you! The first step is to become more mindful of these behaviors, as well as being mindful of the thoughts and feelings that might lead to them. Becoming aware of yourself by becoming a better and *objective* observer of your own behavior is not easy to do. It takes frequent practice. There are a ton of resources, many of which are free, available to help you become more mindful. When you recognize you are getting caught up in your thoughts and feelings and not behaving in ways that move you toward your values, don't be disheartened. It's actually a win because you are aware of it, which is fundamental to mindful practice. If you understand and value this, you will progressively engage in practice as your behavior is positively reinforced. And by this point in the book, we hope you've come to recognize that behavior can be more effectively changed through strategies rooted in positive reinforcement. That means your behavior and the behavior of others. Like a recovering addict, the first step is recognizing and admitting you have a behavior problem.

As Dr. Daniels reminds us in his book *Measure of a Leader* (Daniels & Daniels, 2007), "The intentional search for the impact of your actions sets you apart from those who try to replicate the actions of other leaders." If reading the above signs made you worry about your leadership, this is a really good leading indicator that you are already on the path. Just take any of your "shitty" behaviors, plug them into the ACT matrix under the behavior section that moves you away from your values, think about the thoughts and feelings that might come and lead to those behaviors, and plug those into the bottom left corner, and begin focusing on and committing to the 5 laws and related behaviors we've outlined in this book. They will *definitely* help you to become a better leader of yourself and others.

KEY TAKEAWAYS:

- » We must be aware of our behavior.
- » We must be aware of the impact of our behavior.
- » We must help those we lead to be more aware of their behavior and the impact of it.
- » Behavior is what we say, do, think, and feel.
- » We must have a clear understanding of our values.
- » We must identify behaviors that will move us towards our values.
- » We must identify ways to measure progress that let us know we are moving toward or away from our values.
- » We engage in behaviors that allow us to avoid unwanted thoughts and feelings but simultaneously move us away from our values and goals.
- » Use the 5-second rule to self-initiate behaviors that will lead us towards our values.

ASK YOURSELF:

- » Do you truly know what you value?
- » Are your pinpoints (results and behaviors) aligned with your values?
- » Have you identified the values of those you lead?
- » Are the pinpoints in your organization aligned with the values of your followers?
- » Have you identified salient measures that allow you to know if you are moving towards your values?
- » Are you aware of the impact of your behavior on yourself? How do you know?
- » Are you aware of the impact of your behavior on others? How do you know?
- » Are you helping others you lead become more aware of their behavior and the impact of it?
- » Do you have somebody you report out your progress towards valued goals that will help to keep you on track?
- » Do those you lead regularly report out their progress towards valued goals to somebody to help keep them on track?

CHAPTER 8

Reciprocal Feedback

To this point in the book, you have been armed with pinpointing, goal setting, self-monitoring and report outs. Three of the scientific laws that should be regularly applied to produce positive behavioral karma in your life and the life of others. Now let's dive into the importance of feedback for effectively navigating your chosen course to achieve desired outcomes personally and professionally. Not just any type of feedback, but reciprocal feedback as illustrated in the continuation of our story below.

Reciprocal Feedback – Brett and Paulie's Story

After pinpointing, goal setting, and self-monitoring with report outs, our small division added law number 4, *reciprocal feedback*. We began responding with our own comments and feedback to the daily text message graphic display. The team was receiving daily feedback from our corporate office back in NJ, which served to reinforce progress while also giving each employee tips on how they could further work as a team to increase hours worked and continue to meet their goals. In addition, the team members themselves escalated their feedback to each other on the text threads with tips and behavior hacks that resulted in even more synergy and increases in hours worked. Employees also continued with more and more helpful feedback to each other, and the system took on a life of its own. The corporate office was able to successfully fade back our feedback because the system was self-sustaining without us.

As you can see, the reciprocal feedback as it was used in our story provided a very important and constant source of motivation and guidance. Without feedback, no learning or improvement will occur. But if we are going to further explore how to use reciprocal feedback to produce positive outcomes, we must first under what exactly *feedback* is? Unless you've been living under a rock (which we hope you haven't!), you've probably heard the term feedback before. And if you are like most, if anybody has asked you, "Can I give you some feedback?" it probably comes with a negative connotation, as most of the time the feedback given has to do with telling you what you are doing wrong as opposed to what you are doing right. And if you have a history of receiving feedback related to errors in your behavior or performance, there is a good chance that it evokes a bunch of bad feelings. Under the right conditions, feedback *can* serve as an effective means of correcting behavior or performance. But it also serves many other functions, as illustrated in the following behavior analysis of feedback taken right from the researchers' mouths—well, from their articles!

> It has been suggested that feedback may function similarly to the following: (a) a reinforcer or punisher (Carpenter and Vul 2011; Cook and Dixon 2005; Slowiak, Dickinson, and Huitema 2011; Sulzer-Azaroff and Mayer 1991), (b) an instruction (Catania 1998; Hirst et al. 2013), (c) a guide (Salmoni et al. 1984), (d) a discriminative stimulus (Duncan and Bruwelheid 1985-1986; Roscoe et al. 2006; Sulzer-Azaroff and Mayer 1991), (e) a

rule (Haas and Hayes 2006; Prue and Fairbank 1981; Ribes and Rodriguez 2001), (f) a conditioned reinforcer (Hayes et al. 1991; Kazdin 1989), and (g) a motivational (Johnson 2013; Salmoni et al. 1984) or establishing stimulus (Duncan and Bruwelheide 1985-1986).

Now, that paragraph sounds pretty "sciencey." So let's break the purpose of feedback down into everyday terms for impacting behavior. Feedback might function to do the following:

- Start behavior
- Strengthen or maintain behavior
- Stop behavior
- Prevent behavior
- Teach behavior
- Create a desire for people to engage in behavior
- Increase behavior
- Decrease behavior
- Serve as a reminder regarding behavior

As you can see, there is lots of power in feedback as it relates to behavior. As such, it has the potential to produce big behavioral karma. Thus, it is important that you master the art and science of providing feedback. Before we get into reciprocal feedback as the 4th law, let's explore some very important nuances that should be considered when delivering feedback.

The Art of Tung Fu: Tips for Effectively Providing Feedback

With over a combined three-quarters of a century working to help improve behavior and performance, we've noted a pattern of folks looking for the next best thing for improving outcomes. The funny thing is, everybody already has the most powerful tool in the world, and it's been right under their nose the whole time. That's right, their mouth! The simplest and quickest strategy for improving behavior and performance is through effective feedback. As we noted above, feedback is relatively complex and can be used to impact behavior and performance in a variety of ways. Even your proximity to somebody when providing feedback, or the smallest facial expression, slightest change in tone of voice, or tiniest of gestural movements can impact how your feedback is received. One of the keys to effectively influencing behavior through feedback is to remember, it's not just whatcha say, it's how ya say it and when!

Has anybody ever tried to get you to do something by using a condescending or agitated voice? How did it make you feel? Did you do what they wanted you to do? Did it strengthen your relationship with the person, or make you want to avoid them? If it was your supervisor, were you more likely to work harder, or just get the work done when they were looking in order to avoid being reprimanded? While reciprocal feedback is one of the 5 laws, it's more than just telling people what they need to do more, less, and differently. Feedback can be extremely nuanced and communicate many different things, whether intended or not.

The Behavioral Bank

Think about every interaction you have with a person as being a deposit or withdrawal into a "behavior bank" that directly impacts your relationship with them. Recognizing improved behavior or performance though positive and meaningful feedback is like making a deposit in the bank. Correcting poor behavior or performance is like making a withdrawal. Try to make deposits in the bank with as many meaningful interactions as you can while correcting behavior in a way that only takes a small withdrawal. A powerful behavior hack here that has big behavioral karma should be four-plus positive interactions to everyone corrective interaction, with the corrective interaction being presented in a way that respects the person's dignity and helps them to perform better. If your interaction is coercive, it's akin to taking a major withdrawal from the relationship bank. If you do not have enough positive invested, you will likely incur overdraft fees. In fact, you may go bankrupt! Incidentally, overdraft fees will likely result in countercontrol or more of the very behavior that you are trying to eliminate. Below we'll briefly discuss strategies that are generalizable to interactions with both students and adults. But if you were sorting these behaviors into the ACT matrix, you might list "building relationships" in the bottom right quadrant as a value, coercive behaviors like "issuing demands with an angry voice" in the top left as unproductive behavior, and "4:1 ratio of positive to corrections" in the top right. You would just need to list all the thoughts and feelings that might show up and lead to unproductive behaviors in the top left.

Good communication skills can help you in both your personal and professional life. While verbal and written communication skills are important, researchers continue to find that nonverbal behaviors make up a large percentage of our daily interpersonal communication (e.g., Sauter, 2017). How can you improve your nonverbal communication skills in a way that produces the most positive behavioral karma? The following are some more behavior hacks for nonverbal communication that will enhance your ability to communicate effectively with your students and colleagues.

Brevity

We may be overgeneralizing our thoughts to others, but when folks talk too long, we begin to quickly lose interest! In fact, it won't be long before we begin looking for the quickest escape route. And if we sense that the person communicating to us is attempting to be coercive or condescending in any way, we're probably not hearing a word they are saying, as we're surely crafting our rebuttal, which will definitely be short, but likely not sweet! It's been our experience that brief, meaningful interactions tend to be more effective when attempting to influence behavior, especially when the goal of the feedback is correction.

Body Language

Body language, or kinesics as it is known in certain scientific fields, is incredibly important. Body language are expressive movements taken as symbolic actions which display or emphasize thoughts, feelings, moods, intentions or attitudes, and may be used in combination with, or instead of, verbal communication (Birdwhistell, 1970). Your body is very much like a transmitter that is constantly pumping out signals. You must be aware of these signals and understand their impact on the people around you. Is your body language accurately communicating your intent? For example, as we sat around discussing an upcoming training, a group of employees asked us, "Why do you guys look so angry?" At that moment, we both glanced over into the nearest mirror and realized they were right. We did look angry! The problem is, we weren't. We were just in deep thought and conversation. We'll never know how many times people might have thought we were mad when, in actuality, we were just thinking and planning. Behaviors like crossing your arms and knitting your brows are commonly perceived as coercive and can quickly turn people off or even put them on the defensive. American Psychologist, professor, and pioneer in the study of emotions and their relation to facial expressions, Dr. Paul Ekman (1992), calls some of this body language "micro-expressions." Microexpressions are brief, involuntary expressions that show up on a person's face when they are trying to conceal some emotion and occur more frequently in high stake situations. According to Dr. Eckman, these microexpressions are evolutionary and occur in everybody, often without their knowledge, and are very difficult to detect without the use of some sort of technology. If we all had some sort of way to measure this type of behavior, there would be a lot more clarity in direct communication. However, even though most of us do not possess this type of technology, much of our body language *is* detectable and *can* serve as a powerful source of communication. While you can't control the body language of others, you can manage your own to improve your communication and feedback.

There are times when we must give people feedback that they may not want to hear. When it comes to correcting behavior, try relaxing your body language and addressing misbehaviors in a calm manner. We'll discuss some more tips below in our section on tough talks. But know this: some people may actually want to get you upset. We've seen this occur with some couples as one person seems to derive a sort of satisfaction with getting their significant other riled up. We've also found it very common in children who have been labeled "defiant." When they recognize even the tiniest behavioral cues that indicate you are getting upset, you can be sure that they will quickly "push those buttons" to evoke your reaction in the same way they push buttons on their game controllers. We love those little guys, so smart—boy, do they have us conditioned! Unfortunately, each time our body language, even the smallest micro-expression like the slightest knit of the brow, communicates that we are on the way to losing our marbles, we actually increase the likelihood the child will repeat the very misbehavior that frustrated us in the first place. And they will engage in that behavior again, and again, and again if we continue to respond in the same way. That's some powerful negative behavioral karma right there, as the child is actually being rewarded for their misbehavior through your response. Dispassionate and consistent can be a good approach here, like the teacher from *Ferris Bueller's Day Off*. You remember, "Bueller, Bueller . . ."

Incidentally, one of the most powerful interventions for decreasing the likelihood that somebody will be rewarded or reinforced by signs that you are upset is by fostering meaningful relationships with people by connecting through shared values. Shared values provide a common purpose and serve to align behaviors and strengthen relationships while simultaneously eliminating the reinforcement available for making you upset. In fact, when you share values and have a good relationship, even mild disappointment has great potential to have a major impact on somebody's behavior or performance. Besides, developing and nurturing relationships is likely to increase cooperation and produce positive behavioral karma.

Ninja Behavior

Clearly, many problems occurring between people and across organizations are often simply the result of poor communication that people aren't even aware is occurring. The old saying goes, "Sticks and stones may break my bones, but words will never hurt me." While the saying was likely intended to teach young children to ignore the cutting words of a taunting peer, the fact is, words have the potential to hurt, a lot. Communication can be the most powerful weapon a person wields. It can start wars and sink organizations. Fortunately, it also can act as a powerful salve to comfort those distraught or even rally large groups of people to pursue the greater good (e.g., Martin Luther King advocating for peace and equality). As we noted above, it's not just whatcha say, but howya say it, and when! While words are powerful, elements like body language and tone of voice are oftentimes even more powerful. At times they can be used to hammer home a point; at other times, they can inadvertently remove the focus from the point. So it's very important that you are keenly aware of your body language and tone of voice. Beyond body language and tone of voice, let's take a look at some other things that might impact how your feedback is perceived as a result of behaviors and related variables that are more subtle. In particular, what you aren't saying, or what we like to call *ninja behavior*.

Ineffective communicators are unaware of their certain ninja behaviors and the impact they have; therefore, they put little thought into managing them when delivering feedback. However, the most effective communicators are well aware of these nuances and leverage them to ensure their feedback has the desired impact. In fact, the best leaders employ these subtle ninja behaviors to positively impact those around them in a meaningful way. The good news is, ninja behavior is not mystical. It is, as you guessed, simply observable behavior. Some of these behaviors are obvious. Others are micro-expressions and other subtle behaviors that are stealthy and almost invisible, like a ninja. Master communicators recognize and understand the impact these subtle behaviors have on others. Let's shine a light on a couple of these ninja behaviors lurking in the dark. If you become more aware of their presence, you might be able to understand how they impact those in proximity to you and better employ them in a way that makes your feedback more effective.

Distance

Speaking of proximity, have you ever had somebody speak to you while they are standing too close? How did it make you feel? And how are those feelings impacted by your history with that person? When somebody gets close, our history with them typically dictates whether we perceive this as an invasion of personal space, or a comforting act reserved for those we have deeper relationships with. If you have no history with the person, their close communication might seem more like an intrusion of your personal space. Oftentimes what we consider to be our personal space is dictated by cultural behavior norms. As such, it is important you are aware of your own cultural preference as well as the preferences of the people around you when it comes to proximity.

While standing too close to people can be seen as threatening, standing too far away in some cases can also communicate different things, like disdain or even fear. Under certain conditions, appearing fearful through increased proximity can actually invite the very same behaviors we are fearful of. We used to witness this across some of the high-crime neighborhoods we worked in. Given our combat sports background and years spent living or working across similar neighborhoods, we felt relatively comfortable. We liked to walk through the parking lot and say, "What's up?" or high-five some of the folks on the stairs as we made our way toward the apartment where our client was living. Like instant positive behavioral karma, sometimes we'd get a big smile, or somebody might say something like, "What's up, man?" And like delayed positive behavioral karma, we might later find out that the "word out on the street was" that these guys were "okay." Beyond the positive relationships our approach built, it also likely increased our safety. In contrast, we'd witness new therapists or analysts take great care to remain a "safe" distance from these same folks. They'd park at the other end of the building and use the stairs located furthest away. And when walking by the neighborhood folks, they would look straight ahead and act as if they didn't exist. While this might seem intuitively safe, it might have communicated something different to the locals, like, "You think you are better than us." In fact, under certain conditions, these avoidant behaviors might even inadvertently catch the eye of predators, as this type of behavior, interpreted as fearful by some of them, can paint a bullseye on the back of the unsuspecting. The point is, be aware of your proximity and how it might impact others under different contexts.

Attire

Now, this next approach is not a behavior, but rather the product of it. And we are very guilty as charged. Attire is not one of the areas we've accelerated in. If it were up to us, we'd walk around wearing shorts, a T-shirt, and sandals or sneakers all day long, every day. Don't get us wrong, we dress professionally. But it's typically business casual. We typically aren't trying to dress to impress, as we simply like to feel comfortable. It has always been our greatest hope that folks judge us by the content of our character and the impact of our behavior, not the color and thread of our suit (or lack thereof!); however, we do recognize people are judging us (at least initially) by our attire. This is very typical. We might perceive this to be a cultural faux pas, but it is a cultural norm across business and various conditions in the United States. As such, attire has the potential to communicate all sorts of things to different people. These are things like ability, economic status, education, character, and trustworthiness. Since perception is a reality for many, your dressing behaviors have great potential to influence how others perceive your feedback and respond to you.

There are many cultural norms and contextual variables that influence how your ninja behaviors are perceived. The more you stray from the norm, the more variability there is on how your behavior will be interpreted by others. The point is, your body is like a transmitter that is constantly giving out signals that are being interpreted by everybody around you. As such, it's important you are aware of your ninja behavior.

Reciprocal Feedback in Organizations - Power to the People

When people are self-monitoring and reporting out, they must receive feedback on their performance. Moreover, it's also extremely important to intermittently directly observe them performing in the environment to ensure alignment with values and expectations. There are leadership gurus aplenty who tout the importance of leaders ensuring their employees feel safe, cared for, and that they will be helped when in need. In many organizations, similar values are echoed through sound bites such as, "In our organizations, we place family first," or, "We are a family around here." And that sounds pretty damn enticing if you work at a company plagued by mistrust or feelings of insecurity that typically result from bad leadership practices. But like the old saying goes, "You can't judge a book by its cover." Beyond having inside information from veteran employees in an organization, if you really want to find out how much an employer values their employees, ask about their social validity measures. Gauging whether their heart is in initiatives through practical scientific approaches can better inform efforts beyond standard business result data, which is often too far removed to guide intervention. Given employee performance is at the heart of organizational success, it should go without saying that regularly measuring their satisfaction is absolutely critical.

In our field of behavior analysis, *social validity* is defined as "the degree of acceptance for the immediate variables associated with a procedure or program designed to change behavior" (Carter, 2010). In the clinical world, this typically refers to the degree of acceptance as related to the goals of treatment, treatment procedures, and the effects of treatment (Wolf, 1978). In the organizational world, social validity simply might be thought of as a way to gauge how employees feel about particular goals, their view of the processes and associated behavior they must engage in to achieve those goals, how their performance is managed within those processes, and their view of the resulting outcomes (Carr et al., 2002). And when managers and supervisors use this data to report out their accomplishments to senior leadership, an automated and reinforcing feedback loop can be built into the process, which helps to make the process sustainable. That is, employees' behaviors can be reinforced through the positive outcomes that occur as a result of their feedback; managers or supervisors can be reinforced as a result of observing their accomplishments; senior leaders can use this data as a source of reinforcement for their strategic initiatives, or use it to reinforce those employees, supervisors, and managers; and the CEO can use this data as a source of reinforcement for their leadership.

While social validity measures must be carefully developed and data critically analyzed, the importance of assessing how folks are feeling about "how things are going around here" is undeniable and can be a leading indicator of the success, or lack thereof, of a given initiative and the likelihood of achieving desired goals. In fact, it has the potential to sink an organization as large-scale discontentment on the part of employees can be extremely damaging to performance and outcomes. As we discussed, employees do not judge existing processes based on the intention of leadership, but rather the impact that goals, processes, and manager behaviors have on them and the desired outcomes.

We've seen social validity measures applied across different settings in the form of climate and culture surveys. Unfortunately, too often, these surveys are only provided annually, which is akin to an autopsy. In fact, under these conditions, surveys are seldomly taken seriously by the employee, as leadership rarely acts on the feedback provided. Many employees wouldn't even take the time to complete them, a point regularly highlighted by leadership when we've asked if they survey their employees to see how they are feeling about things. A common response, "Nobody really fills them out, so we don't bother." SODH (that's shaking *our* damn head, for those of you not familiar). Of course, nobody fills them out. Why would they when nothing is done as a result of the collective feedback provided by them! We don't think it takes a behavioral scientist to figure that one out. In fact, at times, we've personally found it quite punishing to give our honest feedback to leaders and then never even have it acknowledged. In some cases, we've actually been punished for the very feedback they've asked for. Leaders, please don't kill the messenger!

At any rate, there must be a way for organizations to regularly seek out feedback from their employees as to how they are feeling about critical initiatives. The frequency of these surveys as a reciprocal feedback tool is especially important in the early stages of an initiative, as it allows for agile responses to potential problems and increases the likelihood the initiative will be successful. If it is discovered that staffs' perceptions are trending in a negative direction, this data can be used quickly to support employees and make adjustments through well-timed communication and action. This data can be used to report out to senior leadership as an accomplishment measure, and future surveys can be provided and used to gauge the success of the intervention as part of a continuous improvement process when necessary.

In our organization, a survey is a place where staff can share positive feedback about their mentors or mentees. In fact, there were so many examples of staff sharing excellent feedback that we wanted to create a way to have this displayed for all staff within the company to see. As such, we implemented a process where all of our administration snaps a picture of the feedback for the week, and then share it weekly on our Facebook culture page. This has created increased employee engagement and company-wide examples of what it looks like to be a high-performing employee in our organization.

When needed, this process helps employees receive immediate support. For example, there was a situation where the survey identified that an employee was struggling. When the executive director reached out, the staff member expressed that he was looking at other job opportunities as a result of the anxiety he was experiencing because of his schedule. The executive team quickly responded and alleviated his anxiety by making some minor adjustments to his schedule. As a result, he decided to stay with us and is currently a high-performing leader as a Board Certified Behavior Analyst within the company who we might have otherwise lost without the weekly check-in.

In another example, the survey identified that a group of employees located in a particular region within the state was feeling isolated and not included in various decision-making opportunities along with leadership. As a result of the feedback obtained through the survey, we created a way for the staff in that region to hold leadership meetings and set up systems for them to have similar meetings, social skill outings, etc. that mimic those of our flagship office location. This gave a whole region an opportunity to create a team of leaders who felt valued and connected.

A weekly survey is a very powerful tool that allows leaders to regularly keep their finger on the pulse of the organization while responding with agility to the needs of the staff. The positive behavioral karma experienced from this simple process includes increased engagement, performance, retention, and ultimately the achievement of desired business results.

Throughout our many years as professionals, we've been part of a variety of social validity measurement endeavors. Many were just lip service at best or a measure of compliance as someone checked the survey off their to-do list. A few had potential, as they were provided quarterly, and the data was shared with staff and acted upon. But this type of feedback as a measure and intervention tool is often too far removed from day-to-day performance to remain agile and effective. If you were driving in the city and your GPS was assessing your location and only providing you feedback every ten minutes, you'd be lost. In order to efficiently drive (your behavior) to reach your destination (your goal), you require a constant stream of feedback. But perhaps through the trial and error of turning down this street or the next and beginning to recognize signs and landmarks, you reach your destination. This is clearly a waste of time and energy. And if the destination isn't really that important to you, you might just turnaround and head home, as the effort isn't worth it! One behavior hack in our organization is the practice of immediate and frequent reciprocal feedback that we provide for the first six weeks of employment. As part of the onboarding process, the newly minted employee gets a mentor who calls them weekly to check-in and engages in "holding their hand" during what can sometimes be a scary time for people. We later thin out the schedule of contact as the employee progresses; however, if they continue reporting a need for support, we don't just drop them after six weeks; we let the data drive our actions! The positive behavioral karma from this simple mentoring process is incredible, as evidenced by improved morale, increased camaraderie, improved quality of services, and exceptional retention rates.

Through this analogy and our discussions to this point on reciprocal feedback, we hope the importance of regular feedback is clear to supporting staff and achieving goals. When we say regular, we don't mean annually or quarterly. The quicker feedback can be obtained and acted upon, the better. Easy-to-collect measures allow organizations to remain agile and stay in front of problems as opposed to having to react to issues, sometimes catastrophic, that they might have avoided. And when feedback is reciprocal, the feedback loop can truly accelerate performance. Feedback is nuanced, can serve several purposes, and can be obtained through a number of means. Getting people to become better observers of their behavior and the impact of their behavior as an immediate source of feedback is a gift that keeps on giving—instant behavioral karma at its finest! Let's take a look at a very simple behavior hack through the story and explanation below that can be used to generate this type of feedback and behavioral karma.

Questioning Strategies to Build Success

The Ultimate Behavior Hack for Leadership and Coaching – Paulie's Story

It's 9:45 a.m. Led Zeppelin's "Lemon Song" is blaring through my stereo system as I head to the gym to train professional fighter and legend Brad "One Punch" Pickett. I've made the seventy-mile journey dozens of times over the years as I've worked with Brad and a variety of fighters in South Florida. I'm running late, I think. "Is that the exit?" I ask myself. "It looks familiar." I was so caught up in the music, I forgot to turn my phone's GPS on. So I grab my phone, tap the microphone on the Google app, and say, "Navigate to American Top Team in Coconut Creek." It does it's quick little calculations and shows me the map, and sure enough, I've passed the exit. So, yes, I'm late and starting to wonder if I've been hit in the head too much. I mean, what kind of a dummy drives to the same place over, and over, and over and still can't remember how to get there?

Well, it turns out, I haven't been hit in the head too much— well, at least I don't think so. And while I freely admit to being a dummy in relation to a variety of topics (hey, don't judge!), this has nothing to do with my intellectual prowess. The fact is, I've become dependent on the GPS. While neuroscientists might suggest I've failed to strengthen neural pathways by engaging in the decision-making processes required to get to the gym, behavioral scientists might simply say I've become prompt dependent. *"Prompt dependence* means that a person responds to the prompts instead of responding to the cues that are expected to evoke the target behavior" (MacDuff et al., 2001). Simply put, a *prompt* is "a temporary aid designed to help somebody respond (behave) correctly when they are learning something." We do it all the time in our everyday life when helping others: "Hey, don't forget to . . ." Once the target behavior successfully occurs, prompting should be gradually faded (Cooper et al., 2007). Unfortunately, people have a tendency to become dependent on the prompting, especially if prompt fading doesn't occur. This results in *prompt dependence*. Over time, this dependency not only prevents people from learning new skills, but also influences the ability to function without support (Mesibov, Shea, & Schopler, 2004). Because I never took note of the various signs, landscaping, structures, or numerous other landmarks within the environment that would act as feedback to guide me in the right direction, I was unable to effectively problem solve or make decisions without my handy-dandy GPS. "Hi, my name is Paulie, and I'm prompt dependent."

You might be asking, "What does this have to do with reciprocal feedback?" Well, everything. You see, good people and leaders help others. But great people and leaders help others to help themselves. Regardless of your role (e.g., parent, leader, wife, coach, supervisor, etc.), folks who are seen as knowledge holders or experts in a given area can often find themselves inundated with others asking them for advice. As such, especially in the professional arena, people who excel in a given area or under different conditions can find themselves bombarded with emails, texts, or perhaps navigating around people who abound with questions, not confident in their own problem-solving and decision-making skills. In short, the leader or coach has inadvertently created prompt dependency, as they've not taught others to help themselves.

The more people are prompt dependent, the less effective and less efficient they are, and the more overwhelmed the leader and coach can become. So what can they do? The solution is easy, but it requires a shift in habits. That is, moving from telling to questioning. If somebody doesn't possess the skill required, they should be trained. Basically, this requires instructing, modeling, and providing them ample opportunities to practice and receive feedback within a safe environment. When coaches train fighters, they have them shadowbox, hit the bag, and run through a variety of drills and combos. Initially, they may tell them exactly what to do, show them exactly what to do, and then have them do it as they shape their performance. But somewhere in there, as they begin independently demonstrating the skills, good coaches shift from telling to questioning. Instead of prompting them, "Keep your left hand up," they ask them, "Was your left hand up during that combo?" Instead of telling them to slip a right hand, they ask them, "What should you do when your opponent throws a right hand?" They are not going to be in the ring or cage with them during the fight. Fighters must respond in milliseconds in a fight. To do this, coaches must build not only their physical skill set but their decision-making ability as well. And good leaders must do the same.

In his book titled *Good Leaders Ask Great Questions*, John Maxwell (2014) suggests that if you want to reach your leadership potential, you need to embrace asking questions as a lifestyle. According to Maxwell:

1. You only get answers to questions you ask.
2. Questions unlock and open doors that otherwise remain closed.
3. Questions are the most effective means of connecting with people.
4. Questions cultivate humility.
5. Questions help you to engage others in conversation.
6. Questions allow us to build better ideas.
7. Questions give us a different perspective.
8. And questions challenge mindsets and get you out of ruts.

And we'd like to add, behaviorally speaking, questions reduce the likelihood folks will become prompt dependent. As we've noted ad-nauseum, people tend to be poor observers of their behavior, poor observers of the environment, poor observers of the impact of their behavior on the environment, and poor observers of the environment on their behavior. Essentially, if we do this under these conditions, then this happens. Or if we're under these conditions, if this happens, then we'll do that. Good questioning strategies allow people to better reflect on the link between their behavior and outcomes so they can better problem solve and make effective decisions. Moreover, questioning provides the opportunity for you to gather the information you might use to better guide your interactions.

So what kind of questions should you ask? Try these to get you started. You might even consider writing them on a sticky note and placing them somewhere as a prompt to help you develop the habit. Once you start asking some questions, try to think of them without looking at the sticky note. We don't want you to become prompt dependent!

- What goal are you focused on today?
- Why are you choosing that particular goal to focus on?
- What specifically are you hoping to accomplish?
- What exactly did you do that worked well?
- What did you learn that you didn't know?
- What were the outcomes?
- What might you have done differently?
- What will you do next?

To generate the most effective positive behavioral karma, your leadership should be purposeful. As a leader of your life or within your organization, you should maximize interactions by using behavior science through questioning to assess why bad things are happening and why good things are happening as well (Gavoni & Weatherly, 2019). This is an important note because if you don't help people to recognize the good things that result from their behavior, they might go away. For example, if you are a parent, and your young seven-year-old spilled water as a result of them playing with their toys next to a table they placed their glass of water on, you might ask the following questions:

1. What exactly did you do that led to the water being spilled?
   - I was swinging a toy with rope on it next to the table and knocked the glass of water over.
2. What occurred as a result of the water being spilled?
   - I cried because I felt bad.
   - Papers on the table got wet.
   - I had to get a towel and clean it up.

- Mommy talked to me.
- I wasn't able to play with my toys while I cleaned up.

3. What might you do more, less, or differently next time? The answers here can vary. Simply asking, "What else?" after each response might get them to problem solve and come up with more solutions.
   - Swing toy with rope elsewhere.
   - Refrain from swinging toy with rope.
   - Place a glass of water in another area.
   - Drink water before playing.

4. Then the next time your seven-year-old goes to get a glass of water during playtime, you might ask:
   - Where will you place the water?
   - Why will you place it there?
   - Where will you play with your toys?
   - How will these options reduce the likelihood you will spill water in the future?

5. Finally, when playtime is over, you might ask:
   - What did you notice as a result of you:
     i. Placing the water elsewhere?
     ii. Playing with the toy elsewhere?
     iii. Drinking the water before playing?

The above questioning strategies increase the likelihood that the child would become more aware and then eventually develop better habits as they relate to playing. There was no need to reprimand. In the above scenario, we can make the reasonable assumption that the child didn't purposely knock over the glass. It was an accident and should have treated as such and used as a teachable moment that created future coachable opportunities. Remember, in our chapter on pinpointing, we discussed the need for performance diagnostics to determine if performance issues are a can't do or a won't do. In this case, there may have been a little of both. For example, perhaps the child hadn't yet developed the skills to safely arrange the environment when playing, or maybe the child was simply unaware of the expectations related to his or her behavior under those specific conditions. Asking behavior-based questions in any situation, as illustrated above, will allow you to better assess and intervene as needed. Not only should you ask questions of those you lead, but you should also get into the habit of asking yourself questions rooted in performance diagnostics when you are failing to perform to a standard.

Brett's Story – Asking Questions Where Truth Might Be Questionable

Errol Doebler is a former Navy SEAL and former FBI special agent who comes with some really great strategies. What I was excited about when speaking with Errol here was about how some of the strategies he's used are very methodical, very planned out, and often relate to processes we use in behavior analysis. So when we spoke, even though he used different terms, we had an immediate synergy, as much of what he shared could be explained succinctly through the science of human behavior. Much of what we chatted about was in line with B. F. Skinner's original vision of using positive approaches to strengthen relationships as opposed to coercion, force, and bullying. What I liked is that some of the strategies he used during his interrogations were just being very direct and honest. Here is a transcript of the story he told me that seems like something out of a movie where he successively interrogated a prisoner in the basement of a dungeon in Kazakhstan using positive strategies rooted in the science of human behavior.

My wife and I, based on the work that we did, ended up in one of the former Soviet Republic's jails that no American or even female had ever been to. We got access to a terrorist who was put away for life. He was not leaving that dungeon. You want to talk about a scene straight out of the movies, that place was it. You know the jails themselves were I don't know how many levels down. We were escorted by a guy with a burlap mask. It was crazy. As we went down, it was a literal dungeon with the rock walls and the moisture dripping down off the walls. It was crazy. And then they brought in the guy. And you know, everybody questioned why we would even waste our time talking to him. And my point was, well, because he has the answers and if the host country is gonna let us do it, why wouldn't we just give it a try? We lose nothing. And so we knew that he and I couldn't have been more on opposite ends of what we believed. But we were both willing to do the same thing to achieve what we believed, and that was to fight and die. So there was mutual respect, and I started the interview out with him, telling him that I understood all the differences between us. And I said, "I appreciate you coming out here, and I'm not sure if you came out here just to stick it in my nose that you have all the things I want to know. And you're not going to tell me, but you still came out." I said, "I appreciate it," and I told him what the purpose of my interview was. I said, "There are a couple of people that I'm interested in that I know you know about, and I want to ask you questions about them. Do you think we can do some work?" And he was like, "What are your questions?" So we had to do a little dance, so we asked some very benign questions. I didn't want to insult him when he didn't tell me the truth right out of the gate. And I had my wife behind me, and she'd kind of whisper in my ear that wasn't accurate. I wouldn't hit him with, "That's a lie," but I let him know, "Well, that's not good, you may want to rethink that one." And I could see he was like, "Okay, so you know the answer and you're not disrespecting me. You're not insulting me." If I needed something, I had to show some level of gratitude for the fact that he was talking to me because there was an area of agreement. Right? We found something that we could talk about.

Using this simple questioning strategy of identifying common values, asking very benign questions to begin with, and then progressively asking more sophisticated questions as trust was built on mutual values resulted in the prisoner sharing very important information with Errol that may have prevented a terrorist attack on New York City. In this behavioral science language, we would call Errol's approach using *behavioral momentum.*

As you can see, asking the right questions in the right way can be very powerful. Especially when you share common values. Across various positions, people come to us all the time to ask questions related to leadership and behavior improvement. They regard us as knowledge holders. When we shifted from telling to questioning, magic happened. People began to realize they had the answers the whole time. They were the knowledge holders, and the solutions were often right under their very noses. Instead of debating some of the merits of our recommendations, even though they were based on science, they started buying in more and seemed to feel empowered as they began implementing and sharing what they discovered they already knew. By using good questions and providing strategic feedback based on the responses, they became better problem-solvers, decision-makers, performers, and influencers. If you are a good leader and you want to become great, make the shift from telling to asking great behavioral questions. And don't forget to ask questions about your own performance and the impact of it as a reciprocal feedback loop. Watch the positive behavioral karma happen for you and for others as a result of this powerful behavior hack.

Giving Tough Feedback

Whether you're a supervisor, manager, teacher, coach, leader, or entrepreneur, the people you work with will make a mistake at some point—and you'll have to address it with them. While most of the time, it's simple stuff, there will be times when the behavior might be unethical, unhealthy, dangerous, or just downright bad for them or the organization. If you don't take action, something bad might happen. On the continuum of bad, it might be as simple as the employee developing bad habits. Oftentimes, doing nothing to performance can be like doing something as the performer thinks it's okay or continues to access reinforcement for undesirable behavior. In addition, undesirable behavior can spread like wildfire through vicarious learning, as other employees think, "Well, shoot, if he can get away with it, I can too." In most cases, it's less nefarious as employees, especially new ones, engage in these behaviors, as it is part of the culture or "the way we do things around here."

Brett's Story

I've often been successful with people responding well to my feedback by the way I set the occasion for it. I always let them know before giving the constructive feedback that I have no reason/motive to tell them something that upsets them or makes them uncomfortable other than the fact that I know it will make both them and me better at what we do (and selfishly make me look good when they succeed). Every action they take reflects on them, the organization, and me, and I'm not giving this feedback to them to cover my ass for human resources documentation. It's not to document something I don't even believe in to make my supervisor happy. I only want them to be better performers, even if they don't work with our company, and I know they will benefit from it. My intentions are purely them first, company second, me last.

We are driven by values and principles, and we absolutely loathe making people feel bad about themselves, but then again, we understand that with controlled pain (like ripping a muscle when weight lifting and it growing back stronger) this painful information will make you a stronger leader, person, and ambassador of these values that will have a ripple effect on thousands of vulnerable people, including you.

Honestly, we really think that a lot of poor performance or bad behaviors can be headed off before they even occur using reciprocal feedback. The problem is, most adults avoid attempting to correct undesirable behavior in other adults. They are usually fine doing it with kids. But it seems like most either avoid it or exclusively focus on it. And if you've ever worked with somebody that only focuses on what folks are doing wrong, you can bet the bank nobody wants to be around them, and they certainly aren't getting the best out of people.

As such, we want to give you a few guidelines for correcting unwanted behavior to improve performance.

#1 Assess Using Evidence-Based Questions

We love looking at performance issues through the *performance diagnostic checklist*. If you remember, it provides questions that allow you to flesh out the root cause of performance issues so you can provide an effective intervention. Sometimes the issue might be a lack of knowledge or skills. Other times it might simply be the performer doesn't understand the why or isn't aware of what they are supposed to be doing instead. Other times they might not be in the habit and just need a reminder, or maybe they just need some equipment or help in developing a process. Then there is the other side, the consequence side. And this might involve a little self-reflection. For example, how often are they being observed and provided positive feedback and corrective feedback? Is the ratio of positive to corrective at 4:1. Or are they being asked to do too many things at once? The point here is this: remember not to assume the performer is just lazy or perhaps that they can do something. The performance diagnostic checklist gives you a list of the right questions for determining what's at the root of performance problems.

#2 Increase the Immediacy of Correction, Not the Intensity

As we mentioned above, doing nothing to behavior can be like doing something. Unfortunately, many folks avoid correcting misbehavior in other adults. Even a crummy boxing coach wouldn't wait for their fighter to get knocked out, so he learns a lesson about keeping his hands up. Instead, he would try to correct the performance immediately to avoid this catastrophe. A good boxing coach wouldn't tell the fighter once in a while to keep their hands up under certain conditions, but rather they would correct consistently and immediately. And if they've taught and prompted it, the coach might require their fighter to give a quick push-up or two to foster some more motivation if they've observed them with their hands down—but not a hundred, just one is sufficient! Oftentimes that's enough to serve as a reminder to get their performance going in the right direction. Unfortunately, instead of increasing the frequency and giving correction immediately, many folks end up increasing the intensity of the consequence in an attempt to punish that bad behavior out of them. In fact, by slowly increasing the intensity of an undesirable stimulus, the results on performance can be counterproductive, as the individual slowly adapts to the unpleasant circumstances. As you know, if increasing the intensity of punishment is done regularly, it is actually likely to generate *negative behavioral karma*. So when possible, catch misbehavior early and often before it falls in the undesirable zone. And of course, don't forget to positively reinforce the desired performance.

#3 Ask Permission

Listen, everybody wants choices. Choices are a powerful reinforcer that can generate strong positive behavioral karma. If you need to deliver some tough feedback, ask the performer if it's a good time to do it. You might say something like, "Nigel, I have some constructive feedback to share with you. Is it okay to share it now?" This is a good way to convey respect. Nine out of ten times they will say yes. However, it literally might be a bad time for them. If it is, ask them for a few options to meet when it's a better time. Getting them to say yes is like a quick win or form of behavioral momentum. And this, of course, is assuming the behavior doesn't need to be addressed immediately because the behavior is unethical or potentially harmful.

#4 Use Pinpoints and Bring Data Whenever Possible

When it comes to correcting behavior, it's important to be prepared with the following:

- A pinpoint of precisely what somebody is doing wrong
- The negative impact that is occurring
- Precisely what they *should* be doing
- The positive impact the desired performance will have

Make damn sure you stick to behaviors, not judgments. Nobody wants to feel judged or feel that they are a bad person. Stick to behavior, and ideally, bring data. When you do this, it leaves you in a completely objective position. Essentially you can let your data do the talking.

#5 Describe the Impact of Their Performance on the Environment

When people don't understand the impact of their behavior on the environment, they may inadvertently behave in ways that lead to undesirable outcomes. It's important they understand and connect their behavior with immediate and distal outcomes they might not directly observe. For example, if a teacher was coming in late and not able to attend her morning supervision post, the principal might say, "I took a look at your time card and was surprised to find you were late three out of five days last week. Unfortunately, when you are late, our supervision is thinned and it sometimes results in an increase in student misbehavior. Just yesterday morning, we had a fight occur in the area you supervise. As I looked at the timecard, I noticed that was a day you were late."

#6 Own Your Mistakes

If for some reason, you play a role, even a small part in their lack of performance, own it! After all, you aren't perfect. Besides, it's a good way to model humility, and it can really serve to strengthen your relationship. When an athlete or team fails, a good coach thinks about what he or she can do differently. The folks you are supervising are like your team. You want them to perform well, so they are successful. So if you've been putting too much on them, or perhaps you haven't been providing enough positive reinforcement or maybe haven't gotten them the resources they need, admit it, apologize, and move on to what you need them to do.

#7 It's Not What You Say, It's How You Say It

Listen, your tone of voice can convey different things. One sentence can have multiple meanings just by accenting one word. For example, take the sentence, "I didn't tell the boss you were late yesterday." Say the following out loud, but put the emphasis on the word we have italicized in each sentence. You will notice that though the words are exactly the same, each sentence communicates something completely different!

- *I* didn't tell the boss you were late yesterday. [Maybe somebody else did.]
- I didn't *tell* the boss you were late yesterday. [Maybe I emailed or texted them.]
- I didn't tell the *boss* you were late yesterday. [Maybe I told somebody else.]
- I didn't tell the boss you were *late* yesterday. [Maybe I told them something else you did.]
- I didn't tell the boss you were late *yesterday*. [Maybe I told them you were late all of those other days.]

Given this illustration, it's easy to see that many times it's not what you say, but how you say it. Having tough conversations with people can be tough. But it's often important for them, the clients, and the organization. And it's also important for you in your everyday relationships. In the end, try not to be too critical or focus too heavily on the negative. The goal of these tough talks and feedback, in general, should be to inspire or reinforce performance, not make the person feel guilty and stuck on where they went wrong.

360-Degree Feedback

In earlier chapters, we talked about positional authority, bad leadership, and the pitfalls of using negative reinforcement or fear of consequences to driving behavior. We even shared some self-assessment tips for determining if your own leadership behavior is $h!tty. It's been our experience that there appears to be a disconnect between many leaders' perceptions of themselves and the perceptions of their followers—even for those who use self-assessments and try to self-monitor. Now at times, this may not be rooted in the reality of the situation. But like the old cliché goes, perception is reality.

> I THINK IT'S VERY IMPORTANT TO HAVE A FEEDBACK LOOP WHERE YOU ARE CONSTANTLY THINKING ABOUT WHAT YOU'VE DONE AND HOW YOU COULD BE DOING IT BETTER.
>
> *- Elon Musk*

As we've noted, employees are not judging leaders by their intentions, but rather by their impact. And if the impact is negative, the achievement of goals is likely low, and attrition of employees likely high. For this reason, there must be a way for leaders to regularly measure their impact upon others. Leaders must seek out feedback on their leadership performance so they know what they are doing well and where they can focus on areas for growth. And if they discover staffs' perceptions are not aligned with the reality of a given situation, leaders can use this data to quickly exercise damage control to reshape perceptions through some well-timed and effective communication.

Whether you are leading an organization or leading your life, you are best served by employing a system of reciprocal feedback. In most systems, feedback typically flows one way, from the top of the org chart down. In this type of system, feedback is provided up, down and laterally throughout your life or throughout the organizational chart to assess and improve performance. This includes leadership performance. In organizations, the 360-degree feedback process is a simple and cost-effective instrument for helping leaders at all levels examine and grow using data based on the perceptions of their followers and others (Luthans & Peterson, 2003).

Essential Questions to Include in Every Leader's 360-Degree Feedback

There are a variety of 360-degree feedback tools on the market. The most effective 360-degree feedback processes provide anonymous feedback that is based on behaviors that other employees can see, and should be used to provide further insight related to the valued skills and behaviors desired to accomplish goals. Whichever you might choose to use, the following questions, firmly planted in critical leadership behavior, should be included as part of any measurement tool for assessing and helping leaders grow (Gavoni & Rodriguez, 2016):

1. My leader provides clear expectations of my role and responsibilities toward the success of the organization.
2. My leader supports me by providing the resources I need to make things happen.
3. My leader enables my professional growth through professional development opportunities, coaching and mentoring.
4. My leader monitors performance and gives me ongoing performance-based feedback, both positive and constructive.

5. My leader communicates to me and my peers consistently about the overall performance of the organization.

6. My leader takes time to directly observe me in action, not to scrutinize, but to optimize my performance.

7. My leader provides ample reinforcement in the form of recognition, positive feedback, and support when I need help.

Please remember, 360-degree feedback should be used as one source of data, not the lone source, as different biases can result in the inflation or deflation of ratings. For example, it's not unusual for people to inflate ratings to make a leader; they like to look good or deflate ratings to make a leader they dislike look bad. In some cases, employees may actually informally band together to make the system artificially inflate everyone's performance. All of these, by the way, might be thought of as examples of behavioral karma, as there is a ripple effect that occurs as a result of their collective behavior. Regardless, checks and balances through other sources of data must exist to prevent these types of pitfalls from occurring.

Incidentally, it's not unusual for employees to be uncomfortable answering questions directly related to leadership, like "What is something the leader can be doing better?" Here is a simple behavior hack for this. When phrased this way, we almost always get a real answer: "What is something you've heard *others* say the leader might be able to do better?" When we ask it this way, employees feel like they are not personally attacking leadership. It may sting a little at first, but honest feedback allows leaders to learn more about what they can do to be better. It may even allow both the recipient of the feedback and the deliverer of the feedback to save face, which allows them to maintain a productive relationship.

It's important to note that this type of measurement and feedback should be employed to help yourself or other leaders grow, not used as a hammer or other tool to demonstrate failure to measure up to leadership expectations (Alimo-Metcalfe, 1998; Edward, 1996). Thus, it is critical for all involved to understand that the 360-degree feedback tool is not an evaluation tool for hiring or firing leaders, but rather a powerful opportunity for leadership development. In fact, those tasked with coaching leadership should also be provided some sort of measurement and feedback related to their effectiveness in coaching!

Whatever type of survey or assessment is used to foster reciprocal feedback, the goal is to either assess or develop SMART pinpoints. To this end, the more specific and relevant your pinpoints are and the more targeted your follow-up is, the more you can help yourself or the people you are supporting develop good leadership habits. Below are a few suggestions (Gavoni & Weatherly, 2019):

- Identify a KPI or key metric and a few behaviors for each individual that manages others. These pinpoints should reflect *support behaviors* or actions that will help others be successful.
- Remember, some of these KPIs should be accomplishments.
- Focus your effort on shaping (you remember, progressively building behavior) to one to two good habits. Ask, "What is the smallest change they can make that will lead to the biggest accomplishment?"
- Schedule time to consistently observe, model, and ask about the one to two habits you are trying to affect.
- Help people see and discuss the impact they are having.

Teaching People to Recruit Feedback

A final note about reciprocal feedback: unfortunately, when it comes to performance improvement in the workplace, people tend to wait for someone to provide feedback. While inputting self-monitoring and report out systems creates a nice feedback loop related to behavior and accomplishments, there are many times people just need more information related to something they are working on, and they don't even know it. Sometimes people fail to ask for feedback because it is delivered poorly or is too often focused on what's going wrong. This can result in the entire feedback process being aversive and create some real Negative Behavioral Karma as the word quickly spreads. When this happens, people will then actually go out of their way to avoid the person and the feedback. In other cases, it's simply that they've not developed the habit of seeking out more information about their performance. Since feedback is critical to learning and performance improvement, this is not good.

An important skill for people to engage in is *recruiting feedback*. This is a powerful skill to be taught (and reinforced) to employees, supervisors, or anybody in a position where providing feedback can help them improve. This applies to you in life and leadership. The frequency with which people seek you out for feedback can actually serve as a measure of your leadership as well as a social validity metric to help you to gauge people's perception and let you know if you are focusing on the right thing in the right way. The nature of reciprocal feedback is that it is a two-way street. Even if you are in a position of authority, you need to constantly make sure what you are doing is having the intended impact. This means you must regularly recruit others' feedback, as we've illustrated in some of the earlier examples.

KEY TAKEAWAYS:

- » Feedback serves many purposes.
- » It's not just about what you say it, but how you say it.
- » Voice, body language, clothing, proximity, and distance impact communicative intent.
- » Ask questions to assess performance deficits.
- » Ask questions to provide the opportunity to provide feedback.
- » Ask questions to help others become better observers of their behavior and the impact of it.
- » Use the 4:1 ratio of positive to negative feedback.
- » Prepare for tough talks.
- » Recruit feedback on your own behavior.
- » Teach others to recruit feedback.

ASK YOURSELF:

- » How often do you provide feedback to others?
- » How often do you recruit feedback?
- » Do you take action based on patterns of feedback?
- » Do you teach others to recruit feedback?
- » When recruiting or teaching others to recruit feedback, do you focus on behavior and impact?
- » Do you link feedback to goals?
- » Do you recognize and give feedback about desirable behavior more than undesirable behavior?
- » Are you aware of how your feedback impacts others?
- » If not, what will you do to measure the impact of your feedback on others?
- » Do you own your mistakes?

» Do you ask permission when you must have a tough talk with somebody?
» Do you increase the immediacy of corrections instead of intensity?
» When having a tough talk, do you let the pinpoints and data guide the conversation?

CHAPTER 9

Pay for Performance

To be successful in life or leadership, you must be in the habit of getting yourself or others "paid" for their behavior. Now we don't necessarily mean money. While money definitely helps in an organization, giving employees more money isn't always reasonable or available. And in your own life, most of what you do likely doesn't result in financial gain, at least not immediately. When we talk of pay, what we are really talking about is getting people in touch with positive reinforcement. Essentially, people need to see the value that occurs as a result of their actions. In this chapter, we will examine pay for performance as it can be applied in an organizational setting and then look at the concept as it applies to your own life. We will also briefly explore punishment and its impact on performance. But before examining these concepts further, let's wrap up the brief story we've illustrated across chapters to highlight the application of pay for performance within one of our company's divisions.

Brett and Paulie's Story

It gets even better with our division of the company increasing their hours worked. After pinpointing, goal setting, self-monitoring, and reciprocal feedback, the team started receiving a small daily monetary reward in alignment with pay for performance. The monetary reward only averaged $10 per day per person, but the impact was phenomenal. The text thread began going viral! The monetary contingency resulted in either *everyone* winning bonuses or *no one* hitting bonuses. We saw team members expressing such gratitude toward each other through statements such as, "I bought my mother that book she always wanted, and she was so happy!" On days they did not reach the goal and receive pay for performance, they would continue cooperating and encouraging each other, making statements like, "We got this tomorrow. We will crush it!"

As you know from the earlier chapter, where we described the importance of reinforcement, most people don't consider it when establishing SMART pinpoints and goals, but the *M* for motivation is extremely important. There must be an establishing operation or a "want" if people are to attempt to engage in pinpointed behaviors that will achieve pinpointed results. The fact that people don't plan for reinforcing consequences upfront is regrettable given that motivation to participate, and reinforcement for performing the required tasks are essential to the success of goal attainment in any setting (Greenberg & Ornstein, 1984). As you've learned, when people get in touch with reinforcement, they will continue to behave or perform in order to achieve the desired outcome. This is why it's so important for people to have skin in the game as the associated accomplishments and outcomes provide lots of reinforcement. We will talk more about having skin in the game shortly. But for now, what's important to understand is that when organizations can make it a win-win, people are engaged in the work, as their behavior, which also adds value to the organization, is naturally reinforced. For example, from presenting at various conferences and universities to developing and sharing articles and videos, we share a ton of content with people. In some cases, like being a keynote speaker, we receive an honorarium. But for most of the content we put out, we are not immediately nor directly paid in terms of cash; however, we both find great value in observing the number of people who read, view, and comment on our work. For us, these are meaningful accomplishments that are leading us toward our ultimate outcome, which is a shared vision: "Expanding the world's collective wisdom of behavioral science to change the landscape of government, education, industry, and society at large."

The reason pay for performance is so often associated with money is that money is one of the most generalizable reinforcers in existence. In other words, it can be used to access all sorts of things that are meaningful to people. However, when money cannot be used, we can still use pay for performance by using function-based reinforcement for behavior. A perfect example is a token system we use that we call Diddy Dollars. Diddy Dollars, provided to employees as a reward for engaging in certain behaviors and achieving particular accomplishments, can be exchanged for a variety of valuable goods and services, and even the opportunity to spin a makeshift wheel of fortune to win cash, which is a favorite. But here's the thing: employees have another favorite. It's not unusual for them to choose another option over spinning the wheel for money. Many actually pick the prize of being able to attend our exclusive Monday leadership meeting. Think about it. Employees actually *valuing* attending a leadership meeting over earning cold, hard cash? The list goes on and on with examples like this and is an indicator of a healthy culture and the outcome of Positive Behavioral Karma established by the relentless contextual application of the 5 laws discussed throughout this book.

Unfortunately, instead of focusing on pay for performance and helping people to have skin in the game to increase accomplishments and outcomes, too often, people tend to use fear of punishment to drive behavior. Instead of having a win-win attitude, their approach might be characterized more like a lose-lose. The problem with this, as you know, is discretionary effort and a ton of other positive outcomes associated with positive reinforcement are squashed. Before we dive a little deeper into pay for performance and a couple of simple behavior hacks for increasing positive reinforcement, let's just do a quick review of problems associated with using fear of punishment to drive behavior (i.e., negative reinforcement). We think it's important to understand the issues associated with punishment, as one can be easily seduced (reinforced!) by the apparent immediate impact of it.

The Negative Behavioral Karma of Punishment - Paulie's Story

As a trainer and consultant, I was giving a workshop to managers on the application of verbal strategies for improving performance. The managers were laughing and joking as I systematically worked through the application of a variety of these strategies to different scenarios. Based on their questions and responses, it seemed like they were engaged and enjoying the training. Moreover, their progressively correct responses let me know they were learning. About halfway through the training (cue the Darth Vader music), the managers suddenly quieted. Where good questions and smiles were only seconds ago directed my way, silence spread like a very unhealthy and contagious virus. "Did I tell a bad joke?" I momentarily wondered. It did not take long to discover the source of the silence. No, it wasn't Darth Vader. And it wasn't me. I am sad to say, it was a member of senior leadership.

After consulting with the company for a short while, it wasn't long before I pinpointed the issue. The leader would walk through the office daily, giving feedback on performance. The problem was, it was focused only on poor performance, which is a damn shame because there was lots of improvement being made. And it was rooted in punishment. That is, telling people what not to do, as opposed to what they should do to be successful. Eventually, the leader's very presence became an undesirable stimulus that just made people feel bad. Even if the leader didn't utter a word, his very presence evoked an emotional response. I remember thinking, "These folks literally look afraid." They were good people. And the leader was probably a good person, but one who just didn't understand how to get the best out of his folks. While some of the employees improved their performance related to the areas they were reprimanded in, most began trying to do a variety of different things to please the leader. After all, the leader told them what not to do, not what they should be doing; moreover, the tunnel vision that resulted from the leader's reprimands only increased performance errors in other areas. And like a bad virus that makes an entire population sick, the negative ripple effect was devastating to the company. Eventually, many of the employees left, and the company almost went bankrupt. And as behavioral karma would have it, the leader got fired.

As we've discussed, the science of human behavior has clearly demonstrated that when fear of consequences drives behavior, people will perform just well enough to get by (i.e., compliance), and typically only when the leader, in this case, the potential deliverer of punishment, is present. In fact, in most organizations, it usually results in staff attrition as folks eventually seek out greener pastures. This is exactly what occurred in the story above. Now there are a variety of reasons staff leave an organization, so if you are a leader reading this who has had a high turnover rate, don't beat yourself up. There are many, many factors that are likely collectively at play, from hiring, onboarding, and standard operating procedures, to training, coaching, and issues associated with evaluations and pay for performance. However, having a fundamental understanding of punishment and the many negative side effects is important, as it is the go-to for many leaders—typically unsuccessful ones.

In Skinner's book *Science and Human Behavior* (1953), he reminds us that punishment typically works to the disadvantage of the person receiving the punishment; in addition, we'd suggest the deliverer of the punishment can experience negative behavioral karma as it can result in side effects like retaliation (you remember, *countercontrol*) and people experiencing debilitating anxiety and escape-motivated behavior (p. 183). All of this can have a performance impeding ripple effect across the individuals and groups you surround yourself with personally and professionally. According to Skinner, "The most important effect of punishment, then, is to establish aversive conditions which are rewarded by any behavior of 'doing something else,'" (p. 189). This is illustrated well in the story above as employees scrambled to engage in behaviors that would keep them from getting in trouble, but most failed to engage in the right behaviors to be successful. Leaders and people, in general, use punishment because it works for them as a negative reinforcer. That is, others will engage in desired behaviors (at least those desired by the person wielding the punishment) that result in the removal of punishment. When a manager yells at somebody for being late and they are on time in the future, this effectively punished late behavior and at least temporarily increased on-time behavior. And this can be fine when used judiciously and in isolation. But when it is the go-to for people, the long-term effects are that it doesn't teach or strengthen a desired behavior, and it results in the negative side-effects cited by Skinner, and for the purpose of this book, negative behavioral karma. Unfortunately, because the wielder of the punishment achieves meaningful results (e.g., think of a dictator getting all his needs met at the expense of his people), they continue to push people past reasonable limits at the expense of both the employee and the outcomes produced. These types of leaders want more, more, and more from those around them. And they might get it because they hold the contingencies as they drive people to work longer and harder, as opposed to smarter. But they definitely are not getting the best out folks.

Overworked and Underperforming - Longer Workdays are Counterproductive

In 1847 Robert Owen (US Socialist) proposed the idea of forty working hours a week and proclaimed the slogan, "Eight hours of work, eight hours of sleep, eight hours of rest," a vast improvement over the ten- to sixteen-hour workdays common to the era (Foner, 1975). While numerous economists have touted the merits of shorter workdays (e.g., Bechtold et al., 1984; Dragone, 2009), many organizations continue to attempt to squeeze productivity out of their workers. Investigations continue to find that fatigue increases cost, reduces productivity, and increases health-related issues. For example, in a recent study of European workers, the share of respondents who stated that their work negatively affects their health rose from 19 percent for those working less than thirty hours per week to 30 percent for those working at least forty hours per week. Other researchers have found weekly working time increases the risk of anxiety, depression, hypertension, cardiovascular disease, chronic infection, diabetes, metabolic syndrome and sleep disturbance (Rodriguez-Jareño et al., 2014; Dembe, Erickson, Delbos, & Banks, 2005).

In some jobs, longer workdays can be very dangerous to both the worker and the consumer. In a study conducted over a period of five years, researchers investigated the effect of shift structure on paramedic performance and productivity (Brachet, David, & Drechsler, 2012). In it, they used approximately 743,000 emergency medical incidents attended by 2,381 paramedics. The researchers determined long work hours and sleep deprivation increase fatigue, which negatively impacts paramedics' performance and increases the likelihood of mortality rates.

In education we've witnessed state officials force struggling schools to increase the school day as a solution to improving student achievement, not getting to the root cause of the issue by taking a deep look at instruction, curriculum assessment, classroom management, processes, systems, equipment, or teacher and leader performance. Just give more of the same the following year and hope for the best. What was it that Einstein said about the definition of insanity? Needless to say, the outcomes have been dismal. It should come as no surprise that the longer people work, the more fatigued and less productive they become. Take a look at the result of this survey that found the average British office worker is only productive for two hours and fifty-three minutes out of the working day. In contrast, research by a New Zealand company found that reducing the workweek from five to four days resulted in a 20 percent increase in productivity, a decrease in stress levels, and an increase in work-life balance scores.

The more people in an organization are disengaged in their day-to-day work, the more negative behavioral karma is generated as evidenced by multiplied absenteeism, low morale, and increased unproductivity as people engage in just enough of the behaviors that will allow them to avoid trouble. What's most important is not the number of hours put in during a workday, but rather the productivity of the employee as evidenced by the number of accomplishments or outputs (Binder, 1998) achieved as it relates to their job. In fact, when you love your work as evidenced by giving discretionary effort as a result of the positive reinforcement produced by your accomplishments, it really isn't like working. This is the best type of pay for performance and produces the greatest amount of positive behavioral karma. Under these conditions, people actually *choose* to work longer. We truly love it when people engage in tasks and activities because they *want* to, not *have* to. The positive behavioral karma generated by this type of leadership and work environment cannot be overstated, and it manifests itself in increased productivity, accomplishments, and outcomes. Often, we personally work (but don't work) sixteen-hour days because our behaviors are under contingencies of positive reinforcement as opposed to contingencies of negative reinforcement; it never feels like work because we are doing this because we *want* to help people versus *having* to help people. Instead of saying we go to "work" every day, it might be more appropriate to say we go "help" daily.

While at times, decreasing the workday makes sense based on the negative impact on productivity, health, etc., it is only a part of the solution. The other part of the solution is increasing performance linked to productivity. Unfortunately, this is complicated by salary, as people are often paid for time spent at work, not productivity, as illustrated by some of the research above.

In his book, *The Sin of Wages* (1996) organizational psychologist Dr. William Abernathy describes the seven sins of the conventional wage-and-salary system, which include some of the following:

1. Fixed-cost pay – wages and salaries are guaranteed, but when revenue declines, the fixed-pay does not. This can put both the organization and the employee at risk. In addition, annual merit raises are often based on time in the organization, not productivity.
2. Pay for time – when people are paid by the hour, it discourages efficiency.
3. Entitlement thinking – because employees are paid for time rather than results, wages and salaries are viewed as entitlement.
4. Management by exception – without objective performance data, people tend to only receive feedback when they make errors, not when they are performing well. This is highly demotivating.

Regrettably, we've personally observed all of these, especially number four! According to Abernathy (2011), the solution, in short, is to design organization-wide performance systems related to (a) sales, (b) expenses, (c) productivity, (d) cash flow, (e) regulatory compliance, (f) customer service, and (g) special projects. The critical results for each category should be used as a measure of performance for each job position and placed in a performance matrix that is shared and discussed regularly with employees. Keeping the performance matrix balanced by measuring and reinforcing performance in areas related to more than just revenue generated has the added benefit of increasing focus on systems, processes, tasks, and behaviors linked to critical outcomes.

For many organizations, Abernathy's pay for performance may be too sophisticated; however, a simple pay for performance approach linked to critical behaviors is the use of accomplishments, as discussed in previous chapters. Instead of positively reinforcing based on outcomes, focus on positively reinforcing based on accomplishments. If the right accomplishments have been chosen, then eventually, they will lead to the desired outcomes. And because the performer doesn't have to wait for the ultimate outcome before receiving some sort of pay for performance, they will continue working toward the ultimate goal. Remember, accomplishments can have a large and positive effect on climate, culture, productivity, and results; moreover, they do a better job of letting both leadership and the performer know they are moving in the right direction. Let's take a quick look at a pay for performance hack we use in our organization to illustrate some of the concepts discussed to this point.

Scanning and Behavior Science to Improve Performance: A Simple Hack

In chapter 3, Gilbert (2007) reminded us that behavior in the workplace is a means, and its consequences, the end. Combined, they make up the performance. In our chapter on pinpointing, we talked about worthy performance. That is, when the value of accomplishments exceeds the cost of behavior in the workplace

(Gilbert, 2007). Behavioral research has shown that well-designed feedback can produce significant improvements in performance that can be accelerated through a combination of goal setting, public posting of performance feedback and tangible reinforcers (Balcazar, Hopkins, and Suarez, 1986). As we've noted, performance is too often only recognized when it falls short, or perhaps when it's too late. Providing feedback and pay for performance at the end of the year as a means of improving performance is useless.

In our organization, and in those we've consulted with, we have come up with a practical way of providing frequent and immediate positive reinforcement for staff for great engagement of social skills with learners across various settings through the use of barcodes and scanners. The process, which has resulted in a large and positive impact on both performance and morale, is fast and reliable and takes far less time than entering data and graphing data by hand. Because a scanner is so easy to use, training folks in the process is simple and inexpensive. And beyond providing data on the performance of staff, it also provides data on the performance of the supervisor in terms of the frequency with which they are providing the scans as a reinforcer. The easy-to-view graphs promote agile decision-making and set the stage for leadership to provide reinforcement to departments, groups, and individuals.

Here's how it works: Since a good part of our staff work with learners who have special needs across multiple settings, we believe it is important to create opportunities that allow for generalization of skills across settings. In other words, a child who learns how to say please or thank you in the home should have the opportunity to say please and thank you in a public setting like a store, restaurant, or another context that is common for individuals and families to be in.

To do this, we have pinpointed very specific behaviors for our staff to engage in on the outings. When excellent performance is identified on a community outing, one of our behavior ambassadors walks up and says something to the staff like, "Awesome job engaging with the learner," and then scans the back of the ID, which has the barcode attached to it. Using the scanner allows for more frequent reinforcement with low effort as it acts as a conditioned reinforcer when the staff feels that they were just recognized for doing something great and they were rewarded for performance. The reinforcement is reciprocated like instant positive behavioral karma as the person providing the scan finds value in reinforcing others. This process is far better than having employees waiting around for a couple of weeks to see if they got some sort of bonus. So the laws of the science of human behavior are executed in an awesome way because pinpointed behaviors are immediately and frequently reinforced in small amounts and the measurement is automatically and immediately collected and graphed, which allows for simple visual analysis of past and present behavior. This immediacy drives peak performance and leads to better outcomes. In this case, our learner's skills generalize more quickly and at a larger scale.

If this sounds great and you are wondering what the process in our organization looks like under these specific conditions, here is the simple procedure we used:

1. The team pinpoints staff behaviors to increase or sustain.
2. Office staff create and distribute barcode (QR codes) labels to fix to the back of every person's ID badge.
3. Behavior ambassadors who supervise events and community supervisors download the app to their phones.

4. The limo team explains to the targeted audience the system and goals that will allow them to access reinforcement.
5. Behavior ambassadors and community supervisors give behavior-specific scans at each event.
6. Scans are posted publicly using an app after each event.
7. A weekly cumulative graph of progress is sent to the participants.
8. Backup reinforcement is provided on a variable schedule.
9. Staff earn T-shirts and move through levels (e.g., like a martial arts belt ranking system) once they receive a certain number of scans.

By using a barcode (QR code) scanner, supervisors can easily provide timely feedback and reinforcement for pinpointed behaviors, that are automatically recorded, graphed, and posted. With the response effort minimized through automation, the process is reinforcing to both the supervisor and the employee. The result, improved quality of services and retention of staff. And listen. If you are a parent, teacher, or coach, this behavior hack is easily generalized to the home, classroom, or gym. If you have the scanner and app, just pinpoint a couple of behaviors you'd like to increase to achieve a meaningful outcome, and you are well on your way to accelerating performance.

Tips for Achieving Skin in the Game

Ultimately, pay for performance is most effective when there is "skin in the game," an idiom that suggests people are invested in achieving a goal because the outcomes directly impact them. Essentially, skin in the game might be thought of as a win-win or lose-lose. Behaviorally speaking, when people have skin in the game, their behaviors fall under contingencies of both positive and negative reinforcement.

Consider a professional football team. The players are invested in training hard and cooperating on and off the field because of all of the amazing valued outcomes associated with performing well and achieving performance goals that lead to valued outcomes like winning games. By the same token, these players are also invested in working hard individually and as a team to avoid poor performance and all of the aversive outcomes associated with losing. These folks aren't just watching, but they are deeply engaged during the day-to-day tasks and activities associated with their position.

When people have skin in the game in your organization, they:
- Use terms like "we" instead of "you" or "them."
- Regularly fly the organization's colors if they are on social media
- Are connected with and participate in activities with other members of the organization outside of the workday
- Are more concerned with performance and accomplishments than hours worked
- Offer to support others, even outside of their department
- Regularly seek out solutions to problems as opposed to problems to solutions
- Seek to better themselves in a way that also benefits the organization

When people have skin in the game, their day-to-day behaviors are driven by the accomplishments produced by themselves and others. Their performance is paid, as they see themselves and others moving toward individual and collective goals that benefit all. You can see examples of folks with skin in the game in extreme situations associated with the military or war, to more benign and simple circumstances like a family working together on a farm to produce outcomes beneficial to each individual and the group as a whole.

As a leader, whether it be in your life or within an organization, here is a couple of pay for performance hacks for gaining skin in the game to increase engagement:

- Use the ACT matrix. Instead of doing it for yourself or with an individual, do it with a group to determine:
  - Values.
  - Shared concerns.
  - Unproductive behaviors that lead away from shared values.
  - Committed behaviors that will move the individual and the group toward the shared values.
  - Value-driven goals.
- When engaging in change initiatives, use principles of institutionalization, which simply means involving the group in the design and implementation of the action plan as an intervention. This can be accomplished by the following (Sigurdsson & Austin, 2006):
  - Training and involvement of in-house staff in developing an action plan.
  - Training of internal staff in the implementation of the action plan.
  - Involving internal staff in collecting data on performance measures and reporting out
  - Involving staff in the dispensing of consequences.
- Providing employees a piece of the pie! Remember, the salary can squash motivation and accomplishments as people end up just doing their time. In our organization, employees can earn up to 5 percent of a contract in perpetuity for their

continued support. This increases the likelihood that not only will they grow contracts, but they will ensure quality services are provided to maintain them! This is a true win-win as the individual, the client, and the organization all benefit.

Capturing the Essence of Pay for Performance

In the end, it's about reinforcement. And when the reinforcement occurs naturally as opposed to literal pay for performance, you or others are more likely to engage in a task because you find some sort of value in it as opposed to contrived reinforcers like recognition, bonuses, etc. Naturally, occurring reinforcement is like the holy grail when behavior adds value to personal goals, professional goals, or organizational goals. However, many times, especially in the initial stages of behavior, contrived reinforcers must be used to get behavior going long enough until success is reached and the naturally occurring reinforcement takes over. Take a child learning to read. Initially, it is likely the encouragement of the adults in the room that maintains their behavior. However, over time, when the child learns how to read, the task of reading becomes a naturally occurring reinforcement. It's just automatic! Contrived reinforcers are often necessary for many behaviors, as people don't love to do everything they have to. And in some cases, as in the case of the child reading, they are necessary when the natural consequences are deferred for a long time. They essentially help to bridge the gap between have to do and want to do.

As we said, it's all about reinforcement—especially positive reinforcement when it comes to getting people to go above and beyond. If you've truly identified SMART goals for yourself and you are regularly self-monitoring, your movement towards those goals serves as pay for performance as your behavior is essentially getting "paid" by the valued outcomes being produced. That is, the reinforcement being produced, as evidenced by movement towards the goals! Here are seven things we want to leave you with regarding reinforcement, some of which is a recap, so you are better able to capture the essence of pay for performance and marshaling the power of positive reinforcement for being a more effective leader of your life or others.

1. Reinforcement is like gravity. Whether you believe it or not, it is constantly happening. As long as you are behaving, reinforcement is occurring.

2. Social reinforcement is one of the most powerful reinforcers in the world. When you treat people kindly and do what you say, you will build trust, help people, and likely spread all sorts of positive behavioral karma that results in you establishing yourself as a powerful positive reinforcer for people. In other words, you are able to positively influence their behavior.

3. Just because you think you are reinforcing somebody's behavior doesn't mean you are. Reinforcement is not defined by the act of giving somebody something. While you might reward yourself or others, that does not mean reinforcement occurred. Reinforcement is defined by its effect on behavior. So the only way to measure whether reinforcement has occurred is if the behavior that preceded the reward increases or is strengthened.

4. Just because you don't think you are reinforcing somebody's behavior doesn't mean you aren't. Sometimes we inadvertently reinforce the behavior we don't want. For example, an adult

who receives attention from you for complaining is more likely to complain to you in the future if he or she values your attention.

5. Just because reinforcement is paired with positive or negative doesn't mean it's about good or bad. It is about change. Positive and negative are about addition and subtraction of something in the environment. It's that addition or subtraction or change in the environment (including your internal environment) that is reinforcing. If you take an aspirin and the headache goes away, the removal of the headache has then negatively reinforced your aspirin taking behavior as evidenced by taking aspirin again in the future. However, removing a headache is probably considered a good thing for most people. Similarly, some people drink alcohol because of the attention they receive while they are with friends and perhaps because of the sense of euphoria they experience from it. This addition of attention and euphoria is considered positive reinforcement if it strengthens or increases their drinking behavior. However, if the person ends up driving drunk or becoming an alcoholic as a result of the positive reinforcement experienced from drinking, most people would consider this bad. I know we do!

6. Some things are naturally reinforcing, like food and water, but many reinforcers are learned. For example, you aren't born wanting to wear fashionable clothing or drive a nice car. However, through your experiences, you've learned to find these things reinforcing. The same with money. It has no inherent value to us; however, we've learned that we can have access to a variety of reinforcers with it.

7. Some things are only reinforcing *sometimes*! For example, if you just threw down a big burger, the likelihood you would hop into your car and seek out more food from the local drive-thru is greatly decreased. We know some people who don't like to drink water because they claim it is tasteless; however, if they're out in the hot sun and haven't had a drink, all of a sudden, a nice cold glass of water is highly valued! Or take dancing. You wouldn't likely break out dancing to your favorite song if you heard it playing in a store in your local mall; however, if that same song was played at the local dance club, you might be much more likely to bust out your moves if you like dancing.

Pay-for-performance is a well-researched concept. But it won't work without the other 4 laws discussed throughout this book. In an organization, the focus shouldn't be on hours worked, but on using the five laws to produce valued accomplishments. When used correctly, the 5 laws can motivate people to join organizations, increase performance, improve morale and retention, and achieve targeted business results. The behavioral principles at the root of the 5 laws can improve outcomes related to city, state, country or even world initiatives. Or they can simply be used to making a meaningful and lasting difference in your daily life. It doesn't matter how much time you or others are putting into something if it is not moving you forward. What matters most is what is being accomplished, and if those accomplishments and consistently moving you or others towards value-driven goals. Whether leading your life or leading within an organization, when pay-for-performance is combined with pinpointing, goal setting, self-monitoring and report out and reciprocal feedback, you've positioned yourself to achieve the most meaningful outcomes possible. This means you are poised to make a positive difference as a leader of your life or as a leader of others. And as you move forward equipped with the 5 laws, know that you've armed yourself with the most powerful science in the world for generating an enormous amount of positive behavioral karma!

KEY TAKEAWAYS:

» Pay-for-performance is about positive reinforcement.
» Driving performance with fear of punishment generates negative behavioral karma.
» Skin in the game is important for sustaining performance.
» It's not about hours worked, but accomplishments produced.

ASK YOURSELF:

» Do I focus more on catching people being good than recognizing poor performance?
» Am I providing people I lead with the opportunity to have skin in the game?
» Do I measure performance based on hours worked or accomplishments produced?
» Do people I lead say "we" instead of "I"?
» When initiating change, do I involve the people I lead in developing an action plan?
» When implementing change, do I ensure the people I lead are involved in the implementation of the action plan?
» Are the people I lead required to collect data on performance and report to me?
» Do I involve the people I lead in delivering reinforcement?
» Am I applying the 5 laws as a leader of my life and others?

SECTION III

The 5 Laws and Crisis

CHAPTER 10

Psychological Safety

To this point, we've led you on a long and winding journey through the 5 laws. From pinpointing and setting goals to making sure you are off to a good start to self-monitoring, reciprocal feedback, and pay for performance to ensure your journey is sustainable, the 5 laws can be applied to every aspect of your life, personally or professionally. There is no doubt about it. Once you view life through a behavioral lens rooted in the 5 laws, you *will* achieve success, and you will help others achieve success as well. Some of the positive behavioral karma that you and those around you will experience is a sense of psychological safety. The power of this is that it continues to feed performance and accelerate the achievement of results. Taking risks is inevitable, but when the risk is too great and people do not feel safe, negative behavioral karma is evidenced by reduced morale, reduced performance, reduced accomplishments, and reduced achievement of valued results. Let's explore the importance of applying the 5 laws to accelerate positive behavioral karma through the creation of psychological safety as our final bon voyage to you.

Creating Positive Behavioral Karma through Psychological Safety

There are leaders who "eat last," a symbolic gesture of a leader's willingness to sacrifice as Simon Sinek (2014) so famously noted. This is positive behavioral karma at its finest! In his work with organizations around the world, Sinek noticed that some teams trust each other so deeply that they would literally put their lives on the line for each other. Other teams, no matter what incentives are offered, are doomed to infighting, fragmentation and failure. Why? The answer became clear during a conversation with a Marine Corps general. "Officers eat last," he said. Sinek watched as the most junior Marines ate first while the most senior Marines took their place at the back of the line. What's symbolic in the chow hall is deadly serious on the battlefield: Great leaders sacrifice their own comfort—even their own survival—for the good of those in their care. Too many workplaces are driven by cynicism, paranoia, self-interest, and blame. But the best ones foster trust and cooperation because their leaders build what Sinek calls a "circle of safety" that separates the security inside the team from the challenges outside.

Brett's Unicorn Story

Simon Sinek did this talk recently, and I thought it was incredible because it resonated with everything that we do in our organization. The talk was about attracting and hiring people who are trustworthy and competent as opposed to those who are toxic. I'd like to add one thing to his point that I've taken from the Navy SEALs.

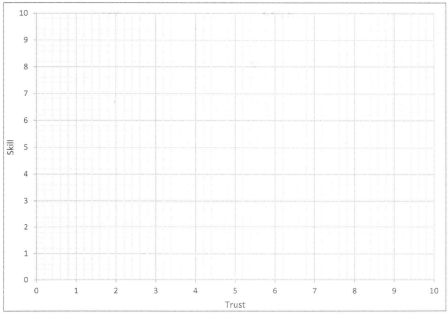

Figure 15: Trust vs. Skill Scale

Both Sinek and the Navy SEALs talk about this on the y-axis, where performance of an employee can be rated from 1–10. If they are extremely competent, they are a 10, extremely incompetent, a 1. Now everybody can't be a 10, but at the end of the day, if they are trending in the right direction, that's what counts. On the X-axis is trust. In other words, if an employee is extremely trustworthy, they are a 10, extremely untrustworthy, they are a 1. Now the Navy SEALs are one of the most elite teams in the world. They obviously know how to go out and conquer all kinds of challenges throughout the world. As an organization focused on helping people through science, I believe we have a similar mission as the SEALS, but clearly without the life-or-death stuff. Now, some people can be highly competent and have really high levels of engagement and performance. This means they could be as high as a 10. However, that same person may only be a 1 or so on the trustworthy scale. As Sinek notes, these people are extremely toxic to the organization or your life. So in other words, it doesn't matter how great you are at what you do if you're not trustworthy. And if you don't feel like you're surrounding yourself with people who are trustworthy, then that person is not only possibly toxic, but they're also potentially very dangerous. Finding someone who is a 10 on engagement and competency and somebody that's also a 10 on trust is almost like finding a unicorn. They hardly ever exist because everyone is good on some days and bad on other days.

When Sinek speaks about this, he says that the Navy SEALs would much rather have someone that falls as a 10 on the trust level but maybe an 8 on the performance level because these are the people who will have the backs of others. They're consistent. They follow through. They deliver what they promise.

When you reverse engineer it and apply it to self-monitoring, when those who are honest self-report, they self-report accurately. When you have people on board you trust and you give some kind of antecedents like a rule, strategy, or suggestion, or perhaps together you set goals, you know they're serious about it and you know that they're going to follow through with it.

In a lot of ways, much of the executive leadership team is like this. We all trust each other 100 percent because we know that if someone's out, we're covering for them and making sure we have their back. Or we know that we're going to make sure we take care of that person's vulnerabilities. Each of us is very much like a puzzle piece that makes up a beautiful puzzle. Some people have really awesome strengths in one area, and another person has a gap in that area. But like a puzzle, we all kind of come together. And although there are hardly any unicorns who are 10 on the trust and competency scale, the trust aspect provides synergy and that keeps that performance scale as close to a 10 as possible through the collective efforts of all.

Whenever we come together, everyone reports out the things they're working on. This is where each person can see how their efforts contribute to the big picture. And this includes when they fill in for somebody else's vulnerability and that person picks up where your vulnerability is. This creates a rock star team and helps our organization transform into one big unicorn. It doesn't matter if people on the team aren't 10s in their competence.

When there is trust, people work together, and their combined effort moves the team to a 10. The point is, whether it be personally or professionally, place more focus on trust over performance and you are far more likely to achieve success.

As this story illustrates, safety, built through trust, can be a powerful tool for strengthening relationships and achieving success. We have been talking a lot amongst ourselves with the behavioral ambassadors we've surrounded ourselves with about the meaning of safety in the workplace. And, as you know, we are not talking about physical safety—more on that in a minute. Somebody made a comment on one of our LinkedIn posts related to behavior analysts in the workplace. And here is what they said: "When did safety become such a concern? When we engage in science, mistakes are welcomed. That's how knowledge is gained and new discoveries made. Are we producing a population of behavior analysts who are afraid to roll the dice for fear that something bad happens to them?" Now, we both absolutely agree that in research, mistakes are welcome. They can and should be learned from. And trial and error under the right conditions is a fantastic way to learn. But that's not what we are talking about. We are talking about creating psychological safety in the workplace, or the overall belief that an employee won't be punished if they make a true mistake. This type of safety, however, one might want to term it, can have lasting positive behavioral karma in many areas like morale, retention, and a variety of other business results. In the case of what our company does, the results quite often happen to be an improvement in the quality of life for children who have special needs. This comment, while likely well-intended, is narrow in scope, in our opinion. And unfortunately, it seems that many people have this kind of "well they need to toughen up" mentality. While that might be the case in the rarest of situations, if you've ever worked for an employer where you felt afraid to make mistakes, then you understand very well that they likely weren't getting the best out of you. And it had absolutely nothing to do with you needing to toughen up. Let's take a deeper look at safety in the workplace.

Many companies proclaim, "Safety is our number one priority." And this is understandable given that OSHA reports the average cost to the workplace industry in 2018 to be about $130,000 per accident. And according to the 2017 Liberty Mutual Insurance Workplace Safety Index, workplace injuries and accidents that caused employees to miss six or more days of work actually cost US employers almost $60 billion. And this has resulted in an $8 billion industry related to improving safety. But this is physical safety. What about psychological safety?

A couple of years back, Google conducted internal research to determine what makes a team perform well. The number one answer listed: psychological safety (Rozovsky, 2015). According to the *Harvard Business Review* (Delizonna, 2017), psychological safety allows employees to take moderate risks, speak their minds, and be creative. The result: innovation, high performance, high morale, and increased camaraderie. And the camaraderie is important to the bottom line. Gallup's State of the American Workplace report (2017) found "when employees possess a deep sense of affiliation with their team members, they are driven to take positive actions that benefit the business—actions they may not otherwise even consider." In fact, the report also found that companies with high engagement experience a 41 percent reduction in absenteeism and a 17 percent increase in productivity, at the very core of high morale, high retention, strong camaraderie, and high productivity: psychological safety.

We've each had the amazing experience of observing, learning from, collaborating with, and consulting with hundreds of leaders over the past two decades. We've personally reaped the benefits of organizations with high morale and strong camaraderie and suffered along with our colleagues in organizations that possessed low morale as a result of the constant fear of punishment. In some fields like education, this has had and continues to have a terrible impact on performance and achievement. For example, in education, some estimates have up to 50 percent of teachers leaving the field inside of five years. And we've seen research that suggests teacher turnover costs anywhere from $7,000 to over $20,000 per teacher and estimates that range from $2 to over $7 billion nationwide. The negative impact on our children and the economy that results from a poor education is immeasurable. And by many accounts, teachers end up leaving schools because they don't feel safe. More specifically, most claim they leave the profession because of the pressures related to both leadership and student behavior. A leading indicator of a lack of psychological safety across these schools and any organization is low morale, which can be easily measured through a variety of social validity surveys.

But low morale doesn't just cost education. It costs businesses, as well. Many researchers have found that it results in regular discontent, poor performance, and absenteeism. Check this out. In 2013, the Gallup Organization estimates there were twenty-two million actively disengaged employees costing the American economy as much as $550 billion per year in lost productivity, including absenteeism, illness, and other problems that result when employees are unhappy at work (Gallup, 2014). Folks, that's $550 billion! Remember earlier, we noted the cost of accidents in the workplace was around $60 billion? Now that is a staggering number in itself. But this is almost ten times the amount! And while there is a thriving $8 billion industry focused on improving safety in the workplace because of the obvious negative impact to the bottom line, psychological safety receives very little attention as the negative impact goes undetected by leaders who fail to make the connection between psychological safety and outcomes related to their mission. What we mean is, it's easy to see that when person X gets hurt, it costs this much money. But the negative behavioral karma is typically much harder to see without regular self-monitoring, report out, and reciprocal feedback.

Listen, we've all heard about our evolutionary fight or flight responses that prompt people to act first and think later. When people feel afraid, they tend to get a kind of tunnel vision that results in hyperfocus on the fight or flight response, and little focus on everything else. In the workplace, this is bad, as people concentrate on what they need to do to avoid punishment. These people do just enough to get by—just like when you are driving on the highway and tend to drive just fast enough to avoid a ticket, and typically only in the presence of the person who will provide the ticket: the cop. This fear suppresses desire and performance and leaves much of the employees' repertoire and creativity untapped. We've seen this manifest itself in wrestling and mixed martial arts (MMA). When a fighter feels unsafe, they will either become very defensive and fail to access their toolbox of offensive weapons, or in the case of MMA, they will begin throwing wild haymakers, end up spending all of their energy, and lose the fight. However, when their defense is solid and they feel safe, it is absolutely amazing to witness the success fighters achieve as a result of their accelerated offensive performance.

Psychological safety is a real thing. It's not just important in businesses and schools either. It's also important in families and relationships and should be regularly measured. Using the 5 laws outlined in this book can help you create this type of safety in your personal and professional life to produce harmony and movement toward individual and shared values. Anybody can do it. It isn't magic, it isn't personality, it isn't charisma, it is simply behavior, the outcomes of which can produce a meaningful ripple effect that you now know as positive behavioral karma.

KEY TAKEAWAYS:

» Psychological safety is critical to performance.

» Fear represses innovation.

» The 5 laws increase psychological safety.

ASK YOURSELF:

» Do I feel safe?

» Do those I lead feel safe?

» How do I know they feel safe?

» Do I put those I lead first?

» Do I do what I say to earn the trust of others?

» Do I surround myself with trustworthy people?

CHAPTER 11

Using the 5 Laws to
Lead During Crisis

As we are wrapping up our book, we find ourselves in the midst of the coronavirus crisis. As unemployment increases, emotional responses like anger, anxiety, fear, and many associated behaviors are rapidly accelerating, as evidenced by protests, arguments, stealing, fistfights in the streets, and increased mental illness and suicide. We are extremely concerned the outcomes of the coronavirus may be much worse than those of the Great Depression in 1929. To navigate this crisis, we do not and will not change our approach. And we recognize more than ever the importance of creating psychological safety during these times. And so should you. You must understand that whatever crisis situation you find yourself in, the 5 laws still apply. You will just need to dive deeper into them and pivot how you apply them.

One of the areas we have been focusing on is ensuring our employees are utilizing the hours available to maximize revenue, sustain employment for all, and ensure the vulnerable learners we serve are receiving quality support. This support was provided primarily through telehealth services, although a small percentage of direct in-home services were provided where it was deemed safe to physically serve in their homes while remaining in compliance with CDC mitigation factors. It is our goal to keep as many people as possible in our organization safe and employed. The other area we are focusing on is keeping our clinic disease-free to keep our vulnerable learners, employees, and their families physically safe. In both cases, we are diving deep into the application of the 5 laws. There is no change in the principles of the 5 laws; however, there are major changes in the way we execute them. For example, we meet and communicate more frequently so we can respond with agility under these turbulent conditions. Shortly, we will take a quick look at where things are to this point through the lens of the 5 laws. Before we do, let's just take a quick tour of leadership again, except this time, leading during a crisis.

Leadership During Crisis

While we've discussed leadership and motivation in earlier chapters, in this epilogue, we think it's important to revisit it given it is absolutely critical to the success of any organization in a crisis. As we detailed in previous chapters, leadership is about influence. Leaders inspire people to feel responsible and accountable for their behavior and outcomes. While inspiration might be thought of as short-term motivation to behave toward a goal, if people are going to continue performing toward that goal, they must find continued meaning in the task and outcome. The best leaders are aware of this and are able to inspire what is known to the behavioral layperson as *intrinsic motivation*. And this is never more critical than when leading through crisis because you, as a leader, will need to instill a certain type of intrinsic motivation, beginning with establishing a strong sense of urgency to adapt to more rapidly changing conditions.

In his book *Leading Change*, Dr. John Kotter outlines an eight-stage model of change, the first of which is establishing a sense of urgency to fight against complacency. In crisis, complacency and the status quo are the enemies of survival. As a leader, you will be asking people to do things more, less, or differently to get through the crisis, which will likely quickly pull them out of their comfort zone. To keep them on track with the many tasks they will likely not want to engage in so that they and the organization can weather the storm, they need a healthy dose of intrinsic motivation. And while establishing a sense of urgency is part of the intrinsic motivation formula, it insufficient for sustainability. But what exactly is intrinsic motivation, how do you get it, and what are some indicators of good leadership that might serve as a measure of this type of motivation?

First off, intrinsic motivation ain't whatcha think! To the behavioral layperson, intrinsic motivation refers to behavior that is driven by internal reward. In other words, the motivation to engage in a behavior arises from within the individual because it is naturally satisfying to him or her. Most people think it comes from inside you. And that's understandable. When you do something that you want to do, you can essentially feel that desire inside you. And that want inside of you can evoke certain behaviors to help you satisfy that want. Right? For example, if you are an artist who likes to paint, you likely have an urge to get in front of an easel and do your thing. The fact that we have bodily sensations that we "tact" or label as urges, emotions, feelings, etc. is not debatable.

We all experience these private events or covert behaviors that we can observe but others can't. But think about intrinsic motivation for one second. What is it that you want? What satisfies that itch? Is it something inside you? Or is it the act of doing something and the outcomes it produces that helps you to feel satisfied and increases the likelihood you will do it again? If you pick up a book, read and enjoy it, the source of your satisfaction is within the book, and you will likely pick it up and read it again and again until the book is completed. In other words, the satisfaction is intrinsic to the task, in this case, reading, not within yourself. Each word and sentence you read engages you and makes you desire to keep reading the next sentence. For one of my professional mixed martial arts fighters, each time they engage in a technique during training, they are rewarded for engaging successfully in the technique by the act itself. Or if they don't perform it correctly, they desire to correct it. Activities like reading and fighting are naturally satisfying to a particular individual. That's why they continue to read the books or train.

So essentially, when we are speaking about intrinsic motivation, what is really meant is the motivation that drives the person's behavior can be found within the task itself. As Komacki et al. (2011) remind us, it's about the consequences. In other words, the behavior is its own reward because of the reinforcement it produces. Behaviorally speaking, Horcones (1983) suggests that intrinsic motivation can be thought of as changes in stimulation produced by the behavior itself. This is in contrast to external motivation or reinforcement that is found outside or extra to the task itself. For example, writing for financial gain as part of a job, as opposed to writing for the personal satisfaction that comes from the finished product, is considered external motivation. The same goes for wearing certain clothing because of the attention it brings from others as opposed to wearing it to stay warm.

However, most behavior is under a confluence of both intrinsic and extrinsic motivation. That is, it occurs because of the different reinforcers it produces that are idiosyncratic to the person. In the writing example above, there might be multiple sources of motivation, like financial gain, the satisfaction of producing a good article, or the positive feedback and attention from others that serve as sources of motivation—or in this case, positive reinforcement. Remember that positive reinforcement simply means that something is added as a result of behavior. This is critical to performance during a crisis because, as a leader, you need all hands on deck going above and beyond to navigate safely through the storm. In many cases, avoiding a penalty (e.g., a professional writer wants to avoid losing pay) might also be thrown into the mix as a source of motivation. This serves as a source of negative reinforcement as people behave to subtract or avoid something unwanted. Remember, when people are driven by negative reinforcement, they will do just enough to get by or avoid that unwanted something.

In crisis, the two types of reinforcement, positive and negative, often work together, as many folks want the organization to be successful while simultaneously they might be concerned about losing their job if they don't perform well. But the greatest leaders inspire and help people feel safe by helping them link their behavior now, even in the most menial task or risky behavior, to a valued future outcome. When people know their job is important, each accomplishment has value and serves to sustain behavior through crises. For example, in a failing school, a good principal helps the cafeteria workers and maintenance personnel understand how their daily work helps to create an optimal learning environment and ties directly into the improvement of student achievement. A more behavior analytic explanation is that the reinforcement value felt by the individual may be directly proportionate to the saliency of each behavior in the chain that leads them to the larger accomplishment. Frequent feedback on each micro-behavior in the form of graphic feedback is an example of this too. The frequent salient feedback all throughout the chain of behaviors can be gradually thinned out so that the individual contacts the final results of their behavior, *resulting in intrinsic reinforcement or meaning* in the complex chain of tasks.

The greatest leaders in history, even during the greatest crisis, have been able to influence people to go above and beyond by helping them find meaning in their day-to-day tasks. In other words, they fostered intrinsic motivation by helping employees experience the task as a source of positive reinforcement. Though the day-to-day task might have been mundane, effortful, or even dangerous at times (as in war), completing it lets them know they were contributing to something bigger, which served as a source of meaning and satisfaction—i.e., positive reinforcement.

Measuring Leadership

While it's extremely hard to determine just how much a leader is fostering intrinsic motivation, in his book *A Measure of a Leader*, Aubrey Daniels (2007) puts forth some simple metrics that can be used as indicators of a leader's influence. Here are some questions to consider about your leader or your leadership. The more you answer yes to these questions, the more likely intrinsic motivation is being cultivated and discretionary performance is being captured.

1. When you know that X is responsible, do you put any extra efforts into his/her initiatives?
2. When X asks you to do something, do you start on it right away?

3. Are you working now on his/her top priority issues?
4. Do you see the connection between your daily efforts and the organization's vision?
5. Can you cite an example of someone living the organization's values?
6. Do you invest as much energy and enthusiasm as the leader invests in his/her initiatives?
7. Can you give a recent example where a peer has helped you with your work?
8. Do other departments and work units cooperate and assist your unit?
9. How many suggestions for improvement have you made within the last three months?
10. Is it safe to admit that you have made a mistake or failed at something?
11. Is X someone you feel you would respect for counsel and advice?
12. Are you actively encouraged to improve your skills and personal growth here?

In the end, we don't think it really matters how intrinsic or extrinsic motivation is defined. The point is, the more a leader can help employees find value in tasks related to organizational goals in a crisis, the more likely they will strive to achieve those goals, even when the leader is not looking. And the more leaders apply the 5 laws during a crisis, the more likely they will be able to work with their team to precisely navigate and weather the storm. If you want to minimize the impact of a crisis on your team or the people you support in any capacity, you must strive to be a leader whose followers answer yes to all of the questions we listed above.

Keeping Our Learners and Employees Physically Safe Using the 5 Laws

According to the CDC, *infection prevention and control* or IPC, is a scientific approach and practical solution designed to prevent harm caused by infection to patients and health workers. It is grounded in infectious diseases, epidemiology, social science and health system strengthening. Since any facility has the potential to be exposed to infectious disease, it is important they are equipped with the tools to prevent the spread of disease. Recommendations by the CDC, like hand washing, environmental cleaning and disinfection, and isolation precautions, are critical to keeping people safe and healthy, especially in these very scary COVID-19 times. Unfortunately, even though many people know exactly what they should do, getting people to actually do it is where the issue typically lies.

Where there is a science for preventing and controlling infection, fortunately, and as you now know, there is also a science of human behavior that can be used to increase the likelihood people will engage in critical behaviors recommended by the CDC. Let's take a look at how we've applied pinpointing, goal setting, self-monitoring and report out, reciprocal feedback, and pay for performance to increase safety for our learners and employees in our clinic.

Pinpointing

Remember, the first law is *pinpointing*. That is, (a) pinpointing the problem (b) pinpointing the result or outcome, (c) and pinpointing the actions that resolve the problem and achieve the desired outcome. Knowing exactly what needs to be done allows you to pinpoint problems when results aren't being achieved and then pinpoint just one or two actions that result in the biggest impact on that problem.

The one or two things you can do, or the one or two things that can be done at scale.

Here were the pinpoints:

» Pinpointed problem – Safety of learners and staff because of coronavirus

» Pinpointed result – Maximize infection and control of facility and treatment integrity related to the CDC guidelines on identified on a checklist

» Pinpointed behavior to achieve result – follow recommendations of CDC (e.g., disinfecting materials and surfaces in targeted areas, washing hands, taking temperatures, wearing masks, and other safety-related behaviors)

Goal Setting

The next law we applied is *goal setting*. Remember, it can be difficult to mobilize people and do anything without a clear goal, and a good behavior is to identify accomplishments as measures of movement toward that goal. When it comes to goal setting to improve infection prevention and control, here is what we did in our clinic:

• Goal: 100 percent daily completion of infection control fidelity checklist by the employee with 100 percent interobserver agreement by supervisor (see appendix).

• Accomplishments:
  - Create the checklist.
  - Put up visual reminders.
  - Complete the checklist at various benchmarks during the day,
  - Turn in the completed checklist at the various benchmarks.

Self-Monitoring and Report Out

The third law is *self-monitoring*. This was especially important because we needed our people to be aware of their behavior because of the possible ramifications of a failure to perform. One of the keys to self-monitoring is reporting out the data to somebody else, which increases the likelihood employees will do what they are supposed to. To self-monitor, the employee was required to do the following:

- Complete the checklist
- Share the completed checklist at designated intervals with supervisor

Reciprocal Feedback

The fourth law is related to feedback. People can report out on what they've done, but it's also important to observe the behavior and results of the employee to let them know how they are doing, as well as a check-in with them to make sure they are being supported. The goal is to improve performance related to infection prevention and control in the clinic through reciprocal feedback. As time passes and treatment integrity improves, this can be faded to intermittent audits more infrequently:

- As the employee completes the checklist, the supervisor observes and completes it as well.
- The employee and the supervisor compare checklists for interobserver agreement.
- If there is a discrepancy in the checklist, the employee and supervisor discuss it and take action where needed.
- The entire checklist is reviewed by the supervisor and the employee at the end of the employees' shift.

- Data is shared weekly on the percentage of completion of the checklist.
- Interobserver agreement shifts from regular direct observation to variable observation through video to reduce observer reactivity and ensure the employee is engaging in the correct behaviors, even when the supervisor is not present.

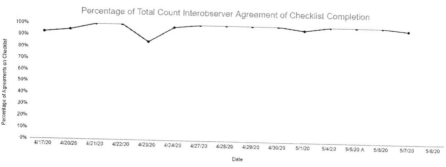

Figure 16: Percent of Checklist Interobserver Agreement

Pay for Performance

The final law that we rounded out the book with is paying for performance. Obviously, people value safety, and you won't need to pay for performance as a bonus for everything. But in this case, we know how extremely important safety is, so we added in pay for performance bonuses for the following:

- Completing the checklist with 100 percent compliance
- Receiving 100 percent interobserver agreement, as the supervisor used the cameras throughout the area to monitor and score the worker

There are a couple of other nuanced details that we didn't cover in the above description, but you get the idea of how we applied the 5 laws to increase safety for our learners and adults within the clinic. Now let's take a look at how we used the 5 laws to sustain employment and continue to support our learners through the initial phases of the coronavirus crisis.

Saving Jobs and Supporting Learners Using the 5 Laws

Our organization serves schools in hundreds of districts across the country. As a result of the coronavirus crisis, in the course of one day, more than half of our employees were out of work because schools shut down. This had a large and negative impact on hundreds of employees and the thousands of learners and educators we serve. We were in a real crisis.

At the time, we were only using around 50 percent of the hours allotted to the learners we were serving in the home. Since most of the learners formerly being served at school were now home, this meant we could shift most of our employees to providing services in the home. But given the restrictions outlined by the CDC, we had to pivot to primarily telehealth options, which essentially meant providing remote support using technology like video conferencing. The biggest issue we had was that we didn't have quite enough hours to keep every single employee on the payroll. While only temporary, we knew we would need to furlough a small group. But who? This was a hard decision to make given the unique situations of each person. We needed to keep the people who were most engaged and willing to pivot to providing telehealth services so we could continue meeting the needs of as many vulnerable learners and their families as possible.

Rather than panic or rely on opinion, we dove right into the application of the 5 laws by creating a system that outlined what work was available and to who we would provide the work. The parameters established for making that determination included the following:

- # of hours previously worked. Those who were maximizing the hours provided to best serve the needs of our learners were prioritized.
- # of learners being served. Those who were providing high rates of direct services to multiple learners were prioritized.
- Compliance with the time system. Those who regularly submitted the number of hours worked were prioritized.
- Mentoring feedback. In our organization, every employee receives mentoring. Data is collected from both the mentor and mentee to ensure satisfaction. Those who were receiving consistent high scores were prioritized.
- Alignment of employee's behavior with organizational values. We are a family first organization. Employees who had children as well as those with special circumstances (e.g., taking care of a sick parent, paying for medical bills, pre-existing illness) were prioritized.

After using these key performance indicators to prioritize, we still showed compassion to each employee by giving them a choice to continue working or for them to initiate unemployment. We accomplished this choice by paying out tens of thousands of dollars of consultation work that was nonbillable to clients so that the employees could still demonstrate work engagement by creating behavior analytic training materials. This was another example of pay for performance when clients were unavailable to work with through telehealth technology. Armed with the parameters listed above, here is how we used the 5 laws:

Pinpointing:

- Pinpointed problem – not enough hours or clients to support the continued employment of 100 percent of our employees
- Pinpointed result – maximizing hours, maximizing learners served, compliance with time system
- Pinpointed behavior to achieve results – directly serve learners through telehealth or create behavior analytic training materials and input hours worked and type of services provided in our time system daily

Goal Setting

At the time, we were only using around 50 percent of the hours we needed to generate as much revenue as possible to keep the organization afloat and continue to employ as many people as possible so we could meet the needs of as many vulnerable learners as possible. So, as a team, we set a goal that was very ambitious:

- 100 percent utilization of hours

Self-Monitoring and Report Out

To monitor progress toward that goal during the crisis, we knew we needed a constant stream of data. Our regular system only allowed for weekly measurement, but we couldn't wait that long. In this crisis, we knew we needed to remain agile, which meant consistent assessment and decision-making using all pertinent data. With the need in mind, Billy Brown, one of our BCBAs and one of our amazing behavioral ambassadors, jumped in and created a system that allowed us to increase the frequency of our self-monitoring and report out processes from weekly to daily. As part of this process, we required employees to report out the following:

- Direct work
- Professional development
- Administrative work

Reciprocal Feedback

I did not have hours today because *

○ 1 - My Clients Canceled

○ 2 - I had to cancel my session

○ 3 - I did not file for unemployment and I need more hours

○ 4 - I filed for unemployment but I am still working & need more hours

○ 5 - I filed for unemployment, but I am working and satisfied with my hours

○ 6 - I filed for unemployment and I'm NOT working because I'm unable to

○ 7 - I did not have time to create ABA content & videos that I can be paid to do

○ 8 - I attempted to enter my hours but the Primepoint system was down

○ 9 - I am part time, satisfied with my hours, and did not have any scheduled sessions today

○ 10 - I am on the admin team, and did not have any hours billable to learners

Figure 17: Google Form Survey

We looked at this data daily and posted feedback in our private company-wide internal social media group with a general thank-you to those who were self-reporting daily. We understood this had increased their effort under conditions that were already producing lots of anxiety, so we remained transparent as we explained we were using the data to maximize employment. If people weren't reporting out hours worked daily, they were sent a Google form survey that had a forced-choice questionnaire. For example:

- I am not on unemployment and I am satisfied with my hours.
- I am not on unemployment and I can use more hours.
- I did not have time to create ABA materials.
- My client canceled.

This also helped us to determine what was in their control vs. what was not in their control. We then had a leader in the organization reach out to every employee based on their response to get more information and then provide them feedback. For example, if an employee replied they needed more hours, one of the leadership team members reached out. When a staff member reported they were satisfied with their hours, it triggered a leadership team member to review their hours utilization. If they were not at 100 percent, the leading member would ask the staff if they could benefit from having additional staff provide support to their learner. If they reported their client canceled, a leadership team member crosschecked that.

Reason	Number of Unique Staff Who Reported Reason
6 - I filed for unemployment and I'm NOT working because I'm unable to	36 (-12)
5 - I filed for unemployment but I am working an satisfied with my hours	29 (-14)
7 - I did not have time to create ABA content & videos that I can be paid to do	27 (-9)
1 - My Clients Canceled	30 (-4)
9 - I am part time, satisfied with my hours, and did not have any scheduled sessions today	29 (-2)
4 - I filed for unemployment but I am still working & need more hours	15 (-3)
2 - I had to cancel my session	17 (+3)

10 - I am on the admin team, and did not have any hours billable to learners	5 (-3)
8 - Primepoint Error	1 (+1)

Reason	Number of Times Reported
6 - I filed for unemployment and I'm NOT working because I'm unable to	152
5 - I filed for unemployment but I am working and satisfied with my hours	75
9 - I am part time, satisfied with my hours, and did not have any scheduled sessions today	81
7 - I did not have time to create ABA content & videos that I can be paid to do	67
1 - My Clients Canceled	53
4 - I filed for unemployment but I am still working & need more hours	33
3 - I did not file for unemployment and I need more hours	38
10 - I am on the admin team, and did not have any hours billable to learners	15
2 - I had to cancel my session	20
8 - Primepoint Error	1

Figure 18: Google Survey Data

When we found employees did not report any hours, we had a leader reach out to them directly. In many cases, employees had initially forgotten, so the call improved our data related to the completion of the Google form almost immediately. The leadership team members were then required to report out at our daily leadership team meeting so decisions could be made based on the data and employee responses.

In the end, analyzing the data daily gave us the information needed to deliver immediate feedback, whether it was to prompt for more hour fulfillment or to provide reinforcement for above-and-beyond performance.

In three weeks, we moved from around 50 percent utilization to 100 percent utilization. We met our goal. As we saw this success and our organization began to stabilize, we began fading the system, from employees reporting out daily to weekly. In addition, we faded the frequency of the leadership team meetings from seven days a week to our current schedule, where we meet and report out on our own pinpoints three days a week.

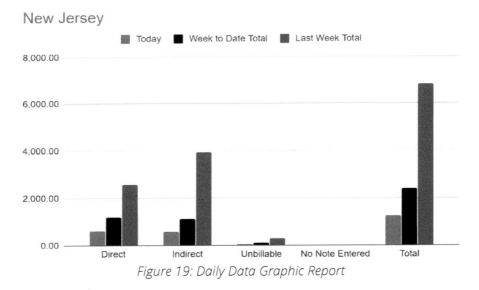

Figure 19: Daily Data Graphic Report

Pay for Performance

In this case, the pay for performance was simple. People who maximized hours, provided the most direct hours to support the needs of the population, had children, or had existing extenuating circumstances were given more weight and maintained their jobs. We also recognized those employees publicly on our internal social media group. In some cases, we even purchased gift cards and other goods to help out their families as an additional bonus. And of course, as an organization, we survived. This was clearly a huge pay-off.

As we wrap up this book, our pivot to telehealth and focus on providing additional services like teletraining and remote coaching has actually allowed us to thrive under conditions where a large chunk of our competitors, unfortunately, has gone under. Our team didn't allow the crisis to control us, alter our values, or change our approach. Rather, we adapted using the 5 laws, generating lots of positive behavioral karma as evidenced by the number of people we were able to keep employed, the number of learners and families continuing to be served, and the positive data that is showing up in our weekly satisfaction surveys. This is a clear example of how we used the 5 laws to appropriately, quickly, and effectively adapt to a changing atmosphere. And the 5 laws can be applied to any situation, anywhere!

Increasing Communication

As you can see, when we initially began to support performance change through the 5 laws, we began by setting shorter goals and requiring more frequent self-monitoring, report outs, and reciprocal feedback to support habit development; however, eventually we faded as the data told a tale of consistently exceptional performance. Whenever we have a performance-based issue, we just keep looking at the problem and the environment, detaching the person from it. We avoid blaming. Instead, we approach the problem through the lens of the 5 laws. In the case of infection prevention and control and maintaining a high level of employment and service delivery, we looked at making adjustments to our pinpoints, goals, self-monitoring and report out, reciprocal feedback, and pay for performance. And then we made it happen!

During a crisis, it's important that you make sure everybody is physically safe. As a leader, it's critical that you remain transparent through the 5 laws as a means of reducing fear, increasing psychological safety, and responding with agility. This requires clear and consistent communication using the 5 laws. And if it is a true crisis, this communication should occur daily. During daily leadership meetings, as problems are pinpointed, actions to resolve them determined, and short-term goals set, members can self-report on the following:

- precisely what they worked on yesterday in relation to the goal
- precisely what they worked on today in relation to the goal
- precisely what they will work on tomorrow in relation to the goal

This is also a time for them to share any impacts on key metrics (graphically when possible), as well as respond to any questions while receiving any helpful feedback from other members. This is what we did in both of the examples illustrated above. We also increased communication by a company-wide shared Google document that gave multiple daily updates about what to expect next, so that an unpredictable situation could be a little more predictable.

Employees who are not able to attend meetings regularly can apply the same principles, but instead of sharing in person, use the approach above to report out through daily emails to their manager or leader. For both in-person and remote communication, all employees should be encouraged to share their immediate needs so they can receive any support required to do their part most effectively during the crisis. While some may see this as micromanagement, it isn't. Communicating frequently allows your organization to respond with agility during a crisis. And transparency builds trust in leadership. As the crisis begins to fade and the performance data trends in the right direction, the frequency of the communication can be faded as well.

Appendix

Performance Diagnostic Checklist

		Training	
Y	**N**	**Description**	**Intervention**
		Has the employee received formal training on this task? If yes, check all applicable training methods: __Instructions __Demonstration __ Rehearsal	The component typically missing is rehearsal. Telling ain't training. If this is missing, training is the appropriate intervention.
		Can the employee accurately describe the target task and when it should be performed?	If they can't tell you how to do it, then they likely need training.
		Is there evidence that the employee has accurately completed the task in the past?	If they've done it successfully in the past, they may simply need a little coaching.
		If the task needs to be completed quickly, can the employee perform it at the appropriate speed?	If they can do it, but not quickly, they simply need to engage in more practice.

Task Clarification and Prompting			
Y	N	**Description**	**Intervention**
		Has the employee been informed that he/she is expected to perform the task?	Many people are unclear about what you expect from them. If they don't know, simply clarify.
		Can the employee state the purpose of the task?	Understanding the *why* of anything is an important motivating factor. If they don't know the why, explain.
		Is a job aid (e.g., a checklist, datasheet) for completing the task visibly located in the task area?	Sometimes it's not that they don't know what to do, but simply they are not in the habit yet. Job aids are practical tools they can use as a guide.
		Is the employee ever verbally, textually, or electronically reminded to complete the task?	Sometimes it's not that they don't want to do it, it's just they forget because they aren't in the habit. A simple reminder can be powerful.
		Is the task being performed in an environment well suited for task completion (e.g., not noisy or crowded)?	This seems like a no-brainer, but this can have a huge impact on performance. Simple environmental adjustments like moving a desk to another area can do the trick.

		Resources, Materials, & Processes	
Y	**N**	**Description**	**Intervention**
		Are there sufficient numbers of trained staff available in the program?	If somebody knows what to do and is motivated to do it, perhaps there's just too much for one person. This must be considered.
		If materials are required for task completion, are they readily available (e.g., easy to find, nearby)?	This is a no-brainer, but having difficulty accessing materials can squash performance. Make sure materials are easily accessible.
		Are the materials necessary to complete the task well designed for their intended purpose?	You can't use a Phillips head screwdriver when a flat head is needed. Make sure the employee has the right materials.
		Are the materials necessary to complete the task well organized for their intended purpose?	A disorganized workspace can increase effort and decrease output. Make sure the employee is organized.
		Can the task be completed without first completing other tasks? If not, what tasks need to be completed first?	If the task is part of a larger process that requires the completion of other tasks prior, help the employee identify and sequence those appropriately.
		If you answered no for the last questions, are other employees responsible for completing any of the earlier tasks in the process? If so, which employee(s)?	Much like a runner in a relay race, as part of a larger process, sometimes the employee's performance might be impacted by the performance of others.

Performance, Consequences, Effort, and Competition			
Y	**N**	**Description**	**Intervention**
		Is the employee ever directly monitored by a supervisor? If so, indicate the frequency of monitoring. ___hourly ___ daily ___weekly ___monthly ___ Other: _____	Simple observation of employees can have a reinforcing effect. Employees who do not have strong habits yet and receive infrequent observation may experience behavioral drift as they fall back into old patterns.
		Does the employee ever receive feedback about the performance? If yes, indicate below. By whom? _____ How often? _____ Delay from task? _____ Check all that apply: Feedback Focus: ___Positive ___ Corrective ___ Feedback Type: ___Written ___Verbal ___Graphed ___ Other: _____	Feedback is at the root of many performance issues. If it's infrequent or overly corrective, it can actually have a negative effect on performance. When it comes to behavior, especially newly acquired behavior, frequent and positive feedback focused on incremental growth accelerates performance. And when performance is graphed, the story it tells can have a large reinforcing effect on future performance.
		Does the employee ever see the effects of accurate task completion? If yes, how?	If the employee is unable to see the positive outcomes of their efforts, they may stop engaging in them. Using the feedback intervention above is a powerful approach here.
		Is the task simple, or does it involve relatively low effort?	Overly complicated tasks or processes can stifle productivity, especially in the early stages of habit development. In these cases, altering the task or improving a process can positively impact performance.
		Does the task generally take precedence over other potentially competing tasks? If not, what are these competing tasks?	If everything is important, nothing is important! As such, taking a look at what tasks take precedence over the task at hand and making adjustments as needed can have a large payoff.

ACT Matrix Worksheet

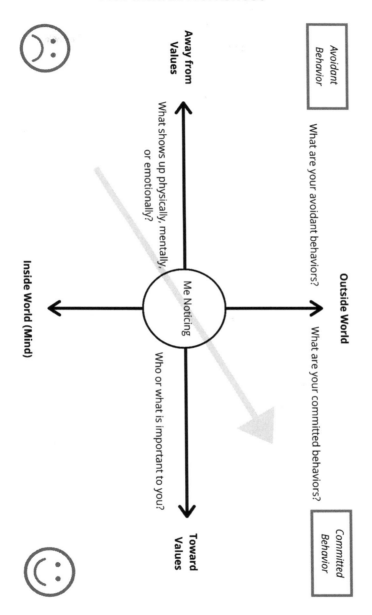

Infection Control Fidelity Checklist

Checklist frequency: Must be completed for each staff member entering the clinic		
Date:	Time start:	Time stop:
Clinical associate name and any other staff present:		
Learner initials:		
Site supervisor:		

Instructions:

Complete the Infection Control Fidelity Checklist as each step is completed to ensure all CDC recommendations are followed through to maximum capacity. This form should be turned into the site supervisor.

Record a:

» Check or mark the box next to each item completed after it is finished. *Some steps may need to be done multiple times (such as handwashing), and a checkmark should be included for every time that this occurs.*

Feedback:

» Feedback will be given both immediately and following the session based on the checklist below.

1. Pre-Arrival of Clients	Checkmark
1a. Staff should wash their hands for at least 20 seconds and take their temperature. Anyone with a temperature of 100 degrees or higher should vacate the facility immediately, and all proper notifications should be made.	
1b. Disinfect all surfaces, materials and workspaces before having a client enter the facility. This includes disinfecting in-between clients. Includes tables, chairs, doorknobs (inside and outside), pens, pencils, light switches, and any other materials that will be used.	
1c. Do not use any materials that cannot be disinfected. Books and paper-based materials are not considered by the CDC to be a high risk for transmission.	

2. Arrival of Clients	Checkmark
2a. Hand sanitizer (60% or higher in alcohol content) should be kept near the door at all times for caregivers dropping the clients off, but they should not be entering the facility, to reduce the number of people inside.	
2b. Staff should meet the client outside of the facility and follow the next steps.	
2c. Prior to the client entering the building, staff should conduct a visual inspection looking for: coughing, difficulty breathing, flushed cheeks or extreme fatigue. Make notes if any of the above appear and make proper notifications and do not allow the client inside the building. See the next step prior to letting the client inside the facility.	
2d. Staff should take the client's temperature outside the facility by implementing the following steps: begin with hand hygiene, then put on a face mask, eye protection, gown/overalls, and a single pair of disposable gloves. Take the temperature and report any temperatures of 100 degrees or higher. Once this is complete, ensure that the thermometer is disinfected. Never use gloves for multiple clients, staff, or other individuals.	
2e. Staff should then escort the client into the building, ensuring they don't touch any surfaces and prompt the client to wash their hands for at least 20 seconds immediately upon entering the facility.	

3. Diaper Changing (if necessary)	Checkmark
3a. Prepare by washing hands, disinfecting all surfaces, and putting on gloves.	
3b. Remove the diaper and clean the client and then remove the gloves.	
3c. Remove all trash, including diapers, wipes, and gloves.	
3d. Replace the diaper and prompt the client to wash their hands for at least 20 seconds.	
3e. Disinfect all surfaces and wash your hands for at least 20 seconds.	

4. Bathroom Visits	Checkmark
4a. Disinfect the bathroom prior to the client entering.	
4b. Prompt the client to use the bathroom as needed.	
4c. Prompt the client to wash their hands for at least 20 seconds.	
4d. Disinfect any area of the bathroom that the client was exposed to.	
4e. Staff should then wash their hands for 20 seconds.	

5. Meals, Snacks, Drinks	Checkmark
5a. Disinfect the area and thoroughly clean any containers that will be used for food or drinks.	
5b. Prompt the client to wash their hands for at least 20 seconds.	
5c. Staff should wash their hands for at least 20 seconds prior to handling any food or drink.	
5d. Staff should then wash their hands for at least 20 seconds, before helping or assisting a client to eat or drink.	

6. On-Going Disinfection (completed throughout the session)	Checkmark
6a. Staff should prompt the client to wash their hands for at least 20 seconds.	
6b. Staff should wash their own hands for at least 20 seconds.	
6c. All surfaces and materials disinfected.	

6. Departure	Checkmark
6a. Staff should prompt the client to wash their hands for at least 20 seconds.	
6b. Staff should wash their own hands for at least 20 seconds.	
6c. Staff should escort the client to the caregiver's car.	

7. Post-Departure	Checkmark
7a. Disinfect all surfaces, materials and workspaces after the client has been escorted from the building. This includes disinfecting in between clients. Includes tables, chairs, doorknobs (inside and outside), pens, pencils, light switches, and any other materials touched.	
7b. Staff should turn this form in to the site supervisor.	
7c. Staff should then wash their hands for at least 20 seconds prior to leaving.	

8. Materials (for site supervisor)	Checkmark
8a. Were thermometers, face masks, eye protection, gowns/overalls, gloves, hand sanitizer, soap and all cleaning supplies stocked?	
8b. Were all materials and supplies disinfected and stored in their proper position?	
8c. Were any materials or supplies replenished (if necessary) following the session?	

9. Preparedness Phase (when there is no known contact with an individual with Covid-19)
9a. Review, update and implement all emergency operations plans (EOP) in collaboration with local health departments.
9b. Develop information sharing with partners.
9c. Teach and reinforce healthy hygiene and increase cleaning/disinfection efforts.
9d. Require any sick staff or clients to remain outside of the facility and advise they stay in their homes.
9e. Review CDC guidelines for business and employers.

10. What to Do Should an Infected Person Be in the Clinic
10a. Coordinate with local health officials.
10b. Dismiss all clients and any staff not necessary for disinfection for at least 2–5 days.
10c. Communicate with all staff and parents.
10d. Clean and disinfect thoroughly.

Clinical Associate Signature: _____

Site Supervisor Signature: _____

References

Abernathy, A., (2014). The liberated workplace: transitioning to Walden three. Atlanta, GA: Performance Management Publications.

Abernathy, W. B., (1996). The sin of wages. *Where the conventional system of pay has led us, and how to find a way out.* Atlanta, GA: Performance Management Publications.

Agnew, J. L. & Redmon, W. K. (1992). Contingency specifying stimuli: The role of "rules" in organizational behavior management. *Journal of Organizational Behavior Management*, 12(2), 67-75.

Agnew, J. L. (1998). The establishing operation in organizational behavior management. Journal of Organizational Behavior Management, 16(2). 7-19.

Alimo-Metcalfe, B. (1998). 360 degree feedback and leadership development. *International Journal of Selection and Assessment,* 6(1), 35-44.

Atkins, P. W., Wilson, D., & Hayes, S., (2019). Prosocial: Using evolutionary science to build productive, equitable, and collaborative groups. Oakland, CA: Context Press.

Austin J. (2000). *Performance analysis and performance diagnostics.* In: Austin J., Carr J. E., editors. Handbook of applied behavior analysis. Reno, NV: Context Press; pp. 321-349. (Eds.)

Austin, J., Kessler, M. L., Riccobono, J. E., & Bailey, J. S. (1996). Using feedback and reinforcement to improve the performance and safety of a roofing crew. *Journal of Organizational Behavior Management*, 16(2). 49-75.

Balcazar, F., Hopkins, B. L., & Suarez, Y. (1986). A critical, objective review of performance feedback. *Journal of Organizational Behavior Management,* 7, 65-89.

Bandura, A. (1997). *Self-efficacy.* The exercise of control. New York: W.H. Freeman and Company.

Baum, W. M. (1994). *Understanding behaviorism: Science, behavior, and culture.* New York: HarperCollins.

Beal S. A., & Eubanks, J. L. (2003) Self-report bias and accuracy in a simulated work setting, *Journal of Organizational Behavior Management*, 22:1, 3-31, DOI: 10.1300/J075v22n01_02.

Biglan, A. (1987). A behavior-analytic critique of Bandura's self-efficacy theory. *The Behavior analyst*, 10(1), 1-15. DOI:10.1007/bf03392402.

Binder C. (1998) The Six Boxes®: *A Descendent of Gilbert's Behavior Engineering Model. Performance Improvement*, 37(6), 48-52.

Binder, C. (2009). *A View from the Top: Human Performance in Organizations.* A white paper from the Performance Thinking Network, available for downloading in the Resource Library at http://www.sixboxes.com.

Binder, C. (2009). Measurement, Evaluation, and Research: Feedback for Decision Making. In Mosley, J. L. & Dessinger, J. C. (Eds.), *Handbook of Improving Performance in the Workplace, Volume 3, Measurement and Evaluation.* San Francisco: Pfeiffer and the International Society for Performance Improvement, 3-24. Available for download at: http://www.sixboxes.com/_customelements/uploadedResources/Measurement_and_Evaluation.pdf.

Birdwhistell, R. (1970). *Kinesics and context: Essays on body motion communication.* Philadelphia: University of Pennsylvania Press.

Bond, F. W. (2004). *Acceptance and Commitment Therapy for stress.* In S. C. Hayes & K. D. Strosahl (Eds.), A practical guide to Acceptance and Commitment Therapy (pp. 275-293). New York: Springer-Verlag.

Bond, F. W., Hayes, S. C., & Barnes-Homes, D. (2006). Psychological flexibility, ACT, and organizational behaviour. *Journal of Organizational Behavior Management*, 26, 25-54.

Brachet, T., David, G., & Drechsler, A. (2012). The Effect of Shift Structure on Performance. *American Economic Journal: Applied Economics*, 4 (2), 219-246. http://dx.doi.org/10.1257/app.4.2.219.

Brigham, T. A. (1980). Self-control revisited: Or why doesn't anyone actually read Skinner anymore? *The Behavior Analyst*, 3(2), 25–33.

Browder, D. M., Liberty, K., Heller, M., & D'Huyvetters, K. K. (1986). Self-management by teachers: Improving instructional decision making. *Professional School Psychology*, 1 (3), 165-175.

Burgio, L. D., Whitman, T. L., & Reid, D. H. (1983). A participative management approach for improving direct-care staff performance in an institutional setting. *Journal of Applied Behavior Analysis*, 16, 37-53.

Byiers, B., Dimian, A., McComas, J., & Symons, F. (2014). Effects of positive and negative reinforcement in a concurrent operants arrangement on compliance and problem behavior. *Acta de Investigación Psicológica*. 4. 1758-1772. 10.1016/S2007-4719(14)70978-0.

Carr, E. G., Dunlap, G., Horner, R. H., Koegel, R. L., Turnbull, S. P., Sailor, W., Anderson, J. L., Albin, R. W., Koegel, L. K., & Fox, L. (2002). Positive Behavior support: Evolution of an applied science. *Journal of Behavior Interventions*, 4, 4-16.

Carr, J. & Wilder, D. (2015). the performance diagnostic checklist—human services: a correction. *Behavior Analysis in Practice*. 9. 10.1007/s40617-015-0099-3.

Carter, S., (2002). *The social validity manual: A guide to subjective evaluation of behavior interventions*. Lubbock, TX: Academic Press.

Catania, A. C. (2007). *Learning* (interim 4th ed.). Cornwall-on-Hudson, NY: Sloan.

Cavico, F., & Mutjaba, B., (2017) Wells Fargo's fake accounts scandal and its legal and ethical implications for management, *AM Advanced Management Journal*, 82 (2).

Comunidad Los Horcones (1992). Natural reinforcement: A way to improve education. *Journal of Applied Behavior Analysis*, 25(1), 71–75. DOI:10.1901/jaba.1992.25-71.

Cooper, J.O., Heron, T.E., & Heward, W.L. (2007). *Applied behavior analysis* (2nd ed.). Upper Saddle River, NJ: Pearson Education.

Daniels, A. C. (1989). *Performance management: Improving quality productivity through positive reinforcement* (3rd ed.). Tucker, GA: Performance Management Publications.

Daniels, A. C. (2000). Bringing out the best in people: *How to apply the astonishing power of positive reinforcement* (2nd ed.). New York, NY: McGraw-Hill.

Daniels, A., & Daniels, D. (2004). *In Performance management: Changing behavior that drives organizational effectiveness.* GA: Performance Management Publications.

Daniels, A., & Daniels, J. (2006). Performance management: Changing behavior that drives organizational effectiveness. Atlanta, GA: Performance Management Publications.

Daniels, A., & Daniels, J. (2007). *Measure of a leader: The legendary leadership formula for producing exceptional performers and outstanding results.* NY, New York: McGraw-Hill.

Dean, M. R., Malott, R. W., & Fulton, B. J. (1983). The effects of self-management training on academic performance. *Teaching of Psychology,* 10 (2), 77-81.

Delizonna, L., (2017). High-performing teams need psychological safety. Here's how to create it. Harvard Business Review https://hbr.org/2017/08/high-performing-teams-need-psychological-safety-heres-how-to-create-it.

Delprato D. J. (2002). Countercontrol in behavior analysis. *The Behavior Analyst,* 25(2), 191-200. DOI:10.1007/bf03392057.

Dembe, A. E., Erickson, J. B., Delbos, R. G., Banks, S. M. (2005) The impact of overtime and long work hours on occupational injuries and illnesses: New evidence from the United States. *Occup Environ Med.* 62:588-597.

Dragone, D. (2009) I am getting tired: Effort and fatigue in intertemporal decision-making. *Journal of Economic Psychology* 30(4):552-562.

Duckworth, A., Peterson, C. D., Matthews, M. D. & Kelly, D. R. (2007). Grit: perseverance and passion for long-term goals. *Journal of Personality and Social Psychology.* 92. 1087-101. 10.1037/0022-3514.92.6.1087.

Edmonds, E., & Gavoni, P., (2017). Experts are made. *Bloody Elbow.* Retrieved from https://www.bloodyelbow.com/2017/6/12/15778472/fight-science-experts-are-made-mma-analysis-film-study

Ekman, P. (1992). Facial expressions of emotion: An old controversy and new findings. *Philosophical Transactions of the Royal Society.* London. **B335** (1273): 63–69. DOI:10.1098/rstb.1992.0008. PMID 1348139.

Fellner, D. J. & Sulzer-Azaroff, B. (1984). Increasing industrial safety practices and conditions through posted feedback. *Journal of Safety Research,* 15, 7-21.

Fellner, D. J. & Sulzer-Azaroff, B. (1984). A Behavioral Analysis of Goal Setting. *Journal of Organizational Behavior Management.* 6. 33-51. 10.1300/J075v06n01_03.

Fellows, C. & Mawhinney, T. C. (1997). Improving telemarketers' performance in the short-run using operant concepts. *Journal of Business and Psychology,* 11(4), 411-424. Experiment 25.

Fischer, W. K., Keller, F., Perruchoud, R. C., & Oderbolz, S. (1993). Light metals, 683-694.

Foner, P., (1975) *History of the Labor Movement in the United States, Vol. 1, From Colonial Times to the Founding of The American Federation of Labor,* International Publishers.

Freeman W. H. and Company. Emory University, Division of Educational Studies, Information on Self-Efficacy: A Community of Scholars.

Gallup (2017) State of the American Workplace. Retrieved from https://cloc.umd.edu/library/research/State%20of%20the%20American%20Workplace%202017.pdf.

Gallup (2014) Report: State of the American Workplace. Retrieved from https://www.gallup.com/services/176708/state-american-workplace.aspx

Gavoni, P., & Rodriguez, M., (2016). *Quick wins! Accelerating school transformation through science, engagement, and leadership.* Melbourne, FL: ABA Technologies.

Gavoni, P., & Weatherly, N., (2019). *Deliberate coaching: A toolbox for accelerating teacher performance.* West Palm Beach, FL: Learning Sciences International.

Geller, E. S. (2003) Leadership to overcome resistance to change, *Journal of Organizational Behavior Management,* 22:3, 29-49, DOI: 10.1300/J075v22n03_04.

Geurin, B., & Foster, T. M. (1994). Attitudes, beliefs, and behavior: Saying you like, saying you believe, and doing. *The Behavior Analyst,* 17, 127-129.

Gilbert, T. F. (2007). *Human competence: Engineering worthy performance*. San Francisco, CA: Pfieffer.

Glenn, S. S. (1988). Contingencies and metacontingencies: Toward a synthesis of behavior analysis and cultural materialism. *The Behavior Analyst,* 11(2), 161–179. https://doi.org/10.1007/bf03392470.

Goal (2019). Businessdictionary.com. Retrieved from http://www.businessdictionary.com/definition/goal.html

Greene, R. (2018). *The laws of human nature.* New York: Viking

Hagopian, L. P., & Jennett, H. K. (2008). Behavioral assessment and treatment of anxiety in individuals with intellectual disabilities and autism. *Journal of Developmental and Physical Disabilities,* 20(5), 467-483. https://doi.org/10.1007/s10882-008-9114-8

Hays, K., Thomas, O., Maynard, I., & Bawden, M. (2009) The role of confidence in world-class sport performance, Journal of Sports Sciences, 27:11, 1185-1199, DOI: 10.1080/02640410903089798.

Hayes, D., Moore, A., Stapley, E., Humphrey, N., Mansfield, R., Santos, J., . . . Deighton, J. (2019). Promoting mental health and wellbeing in schools: Examining mindfulness, relaxation and strategies for safety and wellbeing in English primary and secondary schools: Study protocol for a multi-school, cluster randomised controlled trial (INSPIRE). *Trials, 20*(1), 640. DOI:10.1186/s13063-019-3762-0.

Hayes, S. C., Strosahl, K. D., Bunting, K., Twohig, M., & Wilson, K. G. (2004). *What Is Acceptance and Commitment Therapy?* In S. C. Hayes & K. D. Strosahl (Eds.), A practical guide to Acceptance and Commitment Therapy (pp. 3-29). New York: Springer-Verlag.

Hayes, S. C., Hayes, L. J., Reese, H. W., & Sarbin, T. R. (1993). Varieties of scientific contextualism. Reno, NV: Context Press. al Disabilities. 20. 467-483. 10.1007/s10882-008-9114-8.

Hayes, S. C., Wilson, K. G., & Gifford, E. V. (1999). Consciousness and private events. In B. Thyer (Ed.), *The philosophical legacy of behaviorism* (pp. 153-187). Lancaster, UK: Kluwer.

Hayes, S. C., Wilson, K. G., Gifford, E. V., Follette, V. M., & Strosahl, K. (1996). Experiential avoidance and behavioral disorders: A functional dimensional approach to diagnosis and treatment. *Journal of Consulting and Clinical Psychology, 64*(6), 1152-1168.

Hayes, S. C., Luoma, J. B., Bond, F. W., Masuda, A., & Lillis, J. (2006) Acceptance and Commitment Therapy: Model, processes and outcomes. *Psychology Faculty Publications.* 101.

Heinicke, M. R., Carr, J. E., Leblanc, L. A., & Severtson, J. M. (2010). On the use of fluency training in the behavioral treatment of autism: a commentary. *The Behavior Analyst, 33*(2), 223–229. DOI:10.1007/bf03392221.

Herman, K. C., Hickmon-Rosa, J., & Reinke, W. M. (2018). Empirically derived profiles of teacher stress, burnout, self-efficacy, and coping and associated student outcomes. *Journal of Positive Behavior Interventions, 20*(2), 90–100. https://doi.org/10.1177/1098300717732066.

Hewertson, R., (2014). *Lead like it matters . . . because it does: Practical leadership tools to inspire and engage your people and create great results.* NY: New York: McGraw-Hill.

Horcones. (1983). Natural reinforcement in a Walden Two community. *Revista Mexicana de Analisis de la Conducta, 9*, 131-143.

Hyland, P., Lee, R., & Mills, M. (2015). Mindfulness at work: A new approach to improving individual and organizational performance. *Industrial and Organizational Psychology, 8*(4), 576-602. DOI:10.1017/iop.2015.41.

Janssen, M., Heerkens, Y., Kuijer, W., van der Heijden, B., & Engels, J. (2018). Effects of Mindfulness-Based Stress Reduction on employees' mental health: A systematic review. *PLoS ONE, 13*(1), Article e0191332.

Jebb, A., Tay, L., Diener, E., & Oishi, S. (2018). Happiness, income satiation, and turning points around the world. *Nature Human Behavior.* 2. 33–38. 10.1038/s41562-017-0277-0.

Johnson, S. P., Welsh, T. M., Miller, L. K., & Altus, D. E. (1991). Participatory management: Maintaining staff performance in a university housing cooperative. *Journal of Applied Behavior Analysis, 24*(1), 119-127. DOI:10.1901/jaba.1991.24-119

Kessler, D. L. (1985). The effectiveness of different sources of feedback on outcome and behavior in improving the performance of university baseball pitchers. *Dissertation Abstracts International, 45* (8-B), 2733-2734.

Kipp, M. F., and Kipp, M. A. (2000). Of teams and teambuilding. *Team Performance Management: An International Journal,* 7/8(6), 138-139.

Klein, H. J., Wesson, M. J., Hollenbeck, J. R., & Alge, B. J. (1999). Goal commitment and the goal-setting process: Conceptual clarification and empirical synthesis. Journal of Applied Psychology, 84(6), 885. DOI:10.1037/0021-9010.84.6.885

Komaki, J. L. (1998). *Leadership from an operant perspective.* London, England: Routledge

Komaki, J. L. (1986). Toward effective supervision: An operant analysis and comparison of managers at work. *Journal of Applied Psychology,* 71, 270-279.

Komaki, J. L., Minnich, M. R., Grotto, A. R., Weinshank, B. & Kern, M. J. (2011) Promoting critical operant-based leadership while decreasing ubiquitous directives and exhortations. *Journal of Organizational Behavior Management,* 31:4, 236-261, DOI: 10.1080/01608061.2011.619393.

Laipple, J. (2012). *Rapid change: Immediate action for the impatient leader.* [Kindle DX]. Retrieved from www.PManagementPubs.com.

Langeland, K. L., Johnson, C. M. & Mawhinney, T. C. (1998). Improving staff management in a community mental health setting: Job analysis, training, goal setting, feedback, and years of data. *Journal of Organizational Behavior Management,* 18(1), 21-43.

Lerman, D. C., Addison, L. R., & Kodak, T. (2006). A preliminary analysis of self-control with aversive events: the effects of task magnitude and delay on the choices of children with autism. *Journal of Applied Behavior Analysis,* 39(2), 227-232. DOI:10.1901/jaba.2006.90-05.

Locke, E. A. & Latham, G. P. (1990). *A theory of goal setting and task performance.* Englewood Cliffs, NJ: Prentice Hall.

Locke, E. A., Shaw, K. N., Saari, L. M., & Latham, G. P. (1981). Goal setting and task performance: 1969-1980. *Psychological Bulletin,* 90, 125-152.

Love T. M. (2014). Oxytocin, motivation and the role of dopamine. *Pharmacology, Biochemistry, and Behavior,* 119, 49-60. DOI:10.1016/j. pbb.2013.06.011.

Ludwig, T. D., & Geller, E. S. (2000). Intervening to improve the safety of delivery drivers: A systematic behavioral approach. *Journal of Organizational Behavior Management,* 19 (4), 1-124.

Luthans, F. & Peterson, S. J., (2003) 360-degree feedback with systematic coaching: Empirical analysis suggests a winning combination. Management Department Faculty Publications. 147. https://digitalcommons.unl.edu/managementfacpub/147.

Godat, L., & Brigham, T. (1999) The effect of a self-management training program on employees of a mid-sized organization, *Journal of Organizational Behavior Management,* 19:1, 65-83, DOI: 10.1300/J075v19n01_06

MacDuff, G. S., Krantz, P. J., & McClannahan, L. E. (2001). Prompts and prompt-fading strategies for people with autism. In C. Morris, G. Green, & R. M. Fox (Eds.), *Making a difference: Behavioral intervention for autism* (pp. 37-50). Austin, TX: Pro-Ed.

Maddux, J. (2012). Self-efficacy: The power of believing you can. *The Handbook of Positive Psychology.* 227-287. 10.1093/oxfordhb/9780195187243.013.0031.

Malott, R. (2007). *Principles of Behaviour.* New Jersey: Pearson Prentice Hall.

Malott, R. W. (1992). A theory of rule-governed behavior and organizational behavior management. *Journal of Organizational Behavior Management,* 12(2), 45-65.

Malott, R. W., Malott, M. E., & Trojan, E. (1999). *Elementary principles of behavior.* Upper Saddle River, NJ: Prentice Hall.

Martin, T. L., Yu, C. T., Martin, G. L., & Fazzio, D. (2006). On choice, preference, and preference for choice. *The Behavior Analyst Today,* 7(2), 234–241.

Mawhinney, T. C. & Fellows-Kubert, C. (1999). Positive contingencies versus quotas: Telemarketers exert counter control. *Journal of Organizational Behavior Management.* 19(2).

Mawhinney, T. C. (1992). Evolution of organizational cultures as selection by consequences: The Gaia hypothesis, metacontingencies, and organizational ecology. *Journal of Organizational Behavior Management,* 12(2), 1-26.

Mawhinney, T. C. (In press). Cumulatively large benefits of incrementally small intervention effects: Costing metacontingencies of chronic absenteeism. *Journal of Organizational Behavior Management,* 18(4), 83-95.

Maxwell, J., (2014). *Good leaders ask great questions: Your foundation for successful leadership.* New York, NY: Center Street.

Merriam-Webster. (n.d.). Citation. In Merriam-Webster.com dictionary. Retrieved November 28, 2019, from https://www.merriam-webster.com/dictionary/law.

Michael J. (1993). Establishing operations. *The Behavior Analyst, 16*(2), 191–206. DOI:10.1007/bf03392623.

Miltenberger, R. G., (2004). *Behavior modification: Principles and procedures* (3rd Ed.). Pacific Grove, CA: Wadsworth.

Northouse, P., (2007). *Leadership theory and practice.* Thousand Oaks, CA: Sage Publications, Inc.

Olson, R., & Austin, J., (2001) Behavior-based safety and working alone, *Journal of Organizational Behavior Management,* 21:3, 5-43, DOI: 10.1300/J075v21n03_02.

Olson, R. and Winchester, J. (2008) Behavioral self-monitoring of safety and productivity in the workplace: A methodological primer and quantitative literature review. *Journal of Organizational Behavior Management,* 28: 1, 9-75

Open College UK (n.d.). Retrieved from https://www.opencollege.info/law-of-cause-and-effect/.

Poling, A. & Braatz, D. (in press) Principles of learning: Respondent and operant conditioning and human behavior. In Johnson, C. M., Redmon, W. K., & Mawhinney, T. C. (Eds.), *Organizational Performance: Behavior Analysis and Management.* New York: The Haworth, Press, Inc.

Poling, A., Smith, J. F., & Braatz, D. (1993). Data sets in organizational behavior management: Do we measure enough? *Journal of Organizational Behavior Management*, 14(1), 99-116.

Polk, K., Schoendorff, B., Webster, M., Olaz, F. (2016) *The essential guide to the ACT matrix: A step-by-step approach to using the ACT matrix model in clinical practice.* Context Press, CA.

Prue, D. M. & Fairbanks, J. A. (1981). Performance management in organizational behavior management: A review. *Journal of Organizational Behavior Management*, 3, 1-15.

Rachlin, H. (2002). Altruism and selfishness. *Behavioral and Brain Sciences*, 25, 239–96

Reber, R. A., Wallin, J. A., & Chhokar, J. S. (1990). Improving safety performance with goal setting and feedback. *Human Performance*, 3(1), 51-61.

Redmon, W. K. & Agnew, J. L. (1991). Organizational behavioral analysis in the United States: A view from the private sector. In P. A. Lamal (Ed.), *Behavior analysis of societies and cultural practices* (pp. 125-139). Washington, D. C.: Hemisphere.

Redmon, W. K. & Mason, M. (In press). Organizational culture and behavioral systems analysis. Forthcoming in Johnson, C.M., Redmon, W.K. & Mawhinney, T.C. (Eds.), *Handbook of organization performance: Behavior and management.* New York: The Haworth Press, Inc.

Richman, G. S., Riordan, M. R., Reiss, M. L., Pyles, D. A. M., & Bailey, J. S. (1988). The effects of self-monitoring and supervisor feedback on staff performance in a residential setting. *Journal of Applied Behavior Analysis*, 21 (4), 401-409.

Robbins, M. (2017). *The 5-second rule: Transform your life, work, and confidence with everyday courage.* [Place of publication not identified]: Savio Republic.

Rodriguez-Jareño, M. C., Demou, E., Vargas-Prada, S., et al. European Working Time Directive and doctors' health: a systematic review of the available epidemiological evidence. *BMJ Open* 2014;4:e004916.

Roose, K. & Williams, L. (2017). An evaluation of the effects of very difficult goals. *Journal of Organizational Behavior Management.* 1-31. 10.1080/01608061.2017.1325820.

Rozovsky, J. (2015, November 17) The five keys to a successful Google team. Retrieved from https://rework.withgoogle.com/blog/five-keys-to-a-successful-google-team/

Sauter D. A. (2017). The nonverbal communication of positive emotions: An emotion family approach. *Emotion Review: Journal of the International Society for Research on Emotion,* 9(3), 222–234. DOI:10.1177/1754073916667236

Sigurdsson, S. O. & Austin, J. (2006). Institutionalization and response maintenance in organizational behavior management. *Journal of Organizational Behavior Management,* 26(4), 41-77.

Sinek, S. (2009). *Start with why: How great leaders inspire everyone to take action.* New York, N.Y.: Portfolio.

Sinek, S. (2014). *Leaders eat last: Why some teams pull together and others don't.* New York: Penguin Group.

Skinner B. F. (1974) *About behaviorism.* New York, NY: Vintage Books.

Slade M. (2010). Mental illness and well-being: the central importance of positive psychology and recovery approaches. *BMC Health Services Research,* 10, 26. DOI:10.1186/1472-6963-10-26.

Snyder, M., (1974). The self-monitoring of expressive behavior. *Journal of Personality and Social Psychology,* 30; 526-537.

Spiritual Encyclopedia (n.d.) Retrieved from http://www.spiritual-encyclopedia.com/karma.html.

Strosahl, K., Hayes, S., Wilson, K. & Gifford, E. (2004). *A Practical Guide to Acceptance and Commitment Therapy.* 10.1007/978-0-387-23369-7_2.

Tahmassian, K., & Jalali Moghadam, N. (2011). Relationship between self-efficacy and symptoms of anxiety, depression, worry and social avoidance in a normal sample of students. *Iranian Journal of Psychiatry and Behavioral Sciences,* 5(2), 91–98.

Tamakoshi, B. A. (2014). The association between long working hours and health: a systematic review of epidemiological evidence. *Scand J Work Environ Health,* 40:5-18.

Tarbox, J., Zuckerman, C. K., Bishop, M. R., Olive, M. L., & O'Hora, D. P. (2011). Rule-governed behavior: teaching a preliminary repertoire of rule-following to children with autism. *The Analysis of verbal behavior,* 27, 125–139. DOI:10.1007/bf03393096.

Vargas, E. A. (1988). Verbally-governed and event-governed behavior. *Analysis Verbal Behav* **6**, 11–22 DOI:10.1007/BF03392825.

Wagner, K. (2012, May 30). *Coaching your way to safe habits.* [Blog post] https://www.aubreydaniels.com/blog/2012/05/30/coaching-your-way-to-safe-habits#sthash.C9YtaSMh.dpuf.

Welsch, W. W., Ludwig, C., Radiker, J. E., & Krapfl, J. (1973). Effects of feedback on daily completion of behavior modification projects. *Mental Retardation,* 11,24-26.

Wilson, B., Beamish, W., Hay, S., and Attwood, T. (2014). Prompt dependency beyond childhood: adults with Asperger's syndrome and intimate relationships. *Journal of Relationships Research,* 5, e11 DOI:10.1017/jrr.2014.11.

Winston, A., & Redd, W. (1976). Instructional control as a function of adult presence and competing reinforcement contingencies. *Child Development,* 47(1), 264-268. DOI:10.2307/1128310.

Witt, J., & Beck, R., (1999). *One minute academic functional assessment and interventions.* Longmonst, CO: Sopris West.

Wolf, M. M. (1978). Social validity: The case for subjective measurement or how applied behavior analysis is finding its heart. *Journal of Applied Behavior Analysis,* 11, 203-214.

About the Authors

Brett DiNovi, *MA, BCBA*

Brett DiNovi is a Board Certified Behavior Analyst and the CEO of the largest award-winning behavioral consulting group of its kind on the East Coast of the United States. Brett DiNovi & Associates (BDA) deploys over 450 consultants serving NJ, NY, DE, PA, CA, ME, and internationally through the use of remote video consultation. Brett has the unique and distinguished experience of studying the principles of applied behavior analysis under the rigorous scrutiny of both Dr. Julie

S. Vargas (formerly Skinner) and Dr. E. A. Vargas at West Virginia University's internationally recognized program, and is a member of the Advisory Board for the B. F. Skinner Foundation.

For the past twenty-seven years, Brett has used behavior analytic principles to create large-scale change across school districts and businesses using the principles of organizational behavior management (OBM). Brett has been a consultant in Morgantown, WV, an instructor at West Virginia University, a guest lecturer at numerous universities, a speaker on multiple Comcast Newsmakers TV programs, an expert witness in due process hearings, a contributing writer for online blogs, has publications in the Journal of Applied Behavior Analysis, and has been in executive leadership positions across schools and residential programs nationwide. In addition to an award from *South Jersey Biz Magazine* for Best Places to Work and an award for Best of Families in *Suburban Magazine*, as well as the distinguished Top-Ranked US Executives award, Brett's proudest accomplishment is being a role model and father for his daughter and two stepchildren.

Paul *"Paulie"* Gavoni, *EdD, BCBA*

An expert in human performance, coaching, and organizational leadership, Dr. Paul "Paulie" Gavoni is a behavioral scientist who

has worked in education and human services for over two decades. In this capacity, he served the needs of children and adults in a variety of positions including: COO, Director of School Improvement, Leadership Director, Professor, Assistant Principal, School Turnaround Manager, Clinical Coordinator, Therapist, and Behavior Analyst. As Vice President of Organizational Leadership at Brett DiNovi & Associates, Dr. Gavoni is passionate about applying Applied Behavior Analysis (ABA) and Organizational Behavior Management (OBM) strategies to establish positive and engaging environments that bring out the best in people.

Beyond his work in education and human services, Dr. Gavoni is also a former fighter and highly respected coach in combat sports. Coach "Paulie Gloves," as he is known in the Mixed Martial Arts (MMA) community, has trained world champions and UFC vets using technologies rooted in the behavioral sciences. Coach Paulie has been featured in the books *Beast: Blood, Struggle, and Dreams at the Heart of Mixed Martial Arts, A Fighter's Way,* and the feature article "Ring to Cage: How Four Former Boxers Help Mold MMA's Finest." He is also an author who has written extensively for a variety of online magazines, such as Scifighting, Last Word on Sports, and Bloody Elbow, where his Fight Science series continues to bring behavioral science to MMA.

Known for his authenticity and practical approaches, Dr. Gavoni is a sought-out speaker at a variety of educational, sport, and behavior analytic conferences. Co-author of *Quick Wins! Accelerating School Transformation through Science, Engagement, and Leadership; Deliberate Coaching: A Toolbox for Accelerating Teacher Performance; and MMA Science: A Training, Coaching, & Belt Ranking Guide,* he is proud to introduce the science of human behavior to the world through numerous publications.

Made in the USA
Middletown, DE
24 July 2020